George Smeaton

Learned theologian and biblical scholar

George Smeaton

George Smeaton

Learned theologian and biblical scholar

John W. Keddie

EVANGELICAL PRESS

EVANGELICAL PRESS
Faverdale North Industrial Estate, Darlington, DL3 0PH, England

Evangelical Press USA
P. O. Box 825, Webster, New York 14580, USA

e-mail: sales@evangelicalpress.org

web: http://www.evangelicalpress.org

First published 2007

British Library Cataloguing in Publication Data available

ISBN 0 85234 636 0   ISBN-13 978 0 85234 636 5

Printed and bound in Great Britain by Biddles Ltd., King's Lynn, Norfolk

Contents

Preface

George Smeaton began his *Memoir of Alexander Thomson of Banchory* with this expansive view of the apostolic faith: 'Christianity is destined not only to save the individual, but to fill and ennoble all art and all science, and all literature. Vessels to contain the heavenly treasure, they receive their highest consecration by being made subservient to this end.'[1]

By such a view of the Christian faith, George Smeaton himself, the subject of this biographical sketch, lived.

Besides his invaluable, superb books on the atonement[2] and the Holy Spirit,[3] happily reprinted in recent years, not much is known about George Smeaton. There is a very brief one-page 'sketch' of his life by W. J. Grier in the 1958 reprint of Smeaton's work on the Holy Spirit, and an entry from Ian Hamilton in the *Dictionary of Scottish Church History and Theology* (1993). These rely almost entirely on the Church of Scotland *Fasti* and Free Church *Annals*. No biography of Smeaton ever appeared.

In a lecture at Westminster Theological Seminary in Philadelphia in 1939, Principal John Macleod of the Free Church College, Edinburgh, said that Smeaton's 'work as a theologian still awaits a worthy appraisement'.[4] In a measure this is still true, although there have been several lengthy theses produced on aspects of Smeaton's theology.[5] John Macleod's opinion of Smeaton was that, 'Next to [William] Cunningham, he stood as our foremost student of the history of the Reformed theology.'[6] James MacGregor, a younger colleague of Smeaton's at New College, reputedly said that Smeaton had 'the best-constituted theological intellect in Christendom'.[7]

It is fair to say that until the reprinting of his foremost works in the second part of the twentieth century, next to

nothing would be known in church circles about Smeaton or
his views. The first reprint of his work in the twentieth century
was *The Doctrine of the Atonement as Taught by Christ
Himself*, produced by Zondervan in 1953.[8] Around that same
time an American student, Homer Lehr Goddard, produced a
PhD thesis at Edinburgh University on 'The contribution of
George Smeaton (1814-89) to theological thought'. In his
thesis Goddard covers four areas of Smeaton's thought —
inspiration, the atonement, church and state, and the Holy
Spirit. It is the only thesis so far that has sought to cover all
the important aspects of George Smeaton's work. Though
Goddard is broadly sympathetic in his examination of the
subject, he does not approach his task from a distinctly
conservative standpoint, but rather as one who is happy with
at least some of the tenets of modern biblical criticism and
liberal theology.[9]

Subsequently there have been at least three other doctoral
theses focussing, at least in part, on the theological writings of
George Smeaton. The most thorough of these is the PhD
thesis entitled 'Atonement and pneumatology: a study in the
theology of George Smeaton', by Norman Paul Madsen and
submitted to the University of St Andrews in 1974. In this
work of 343 pages, Madsen deals very thoroughly — and on
the whole helpfully — with Smeaton's theology, especially in
relation to the atonement and the work of the Holy Spirit.
Much of his analysis, however, is taken up with comparing
and contrasting Smeaton's theology in these areas with the
views of Karl Barth and Emil Brunner, and in general with
neo-orthodox theologians. It is clear that Madsen would have
liked more recognition to have been given by Smeaton to the
'human subject' in his theological activity and not so much to
have 'confined himself to the scriptural witness'.[10] Smeaton's
concern, however, was 'not to go beyond the scope of the
scriptural books in formulating his evangelical theology'.[11] He
cannot be pressed into a neo-orthodox mould.

The most recent doctoral thesis on the theological thought of George Smeaton is Robert Shillaker's, 'The federal pneumatology of George Smeaton (1814-89)', produced in 2002. It is clear that Shillaker writes from the same Reformed theological tradition as Smeaton. It is a detailed piece of work which focuses on some central themes in Smeaton's theological position. He covers some areas related to what is called federal theology and the work of the Holy Spirit in relation to these areas. What is meant by federal theology was well stated by Smeaton himself: 'It is due to the federal theology to state that it was only meant to ground and establish the undoubtedly scriptural doctrine of the two Adams (Rom. 5:12-20; 1 Cor. 15:47)... No one can doubt, who examines the federal theology, that the design of those who brought that scheme of thought into general reception in the Reformed church for two centuries was principally to ground, and to put on a sure basis, the idea of the two Adams; that is, to show that there were, in reality, only two men in history, and only two great facts on which the fortunes of the race hinged.'[12]

'What this means,' says Shillaker, 'is that when Adam sinned and fell, soon after his creation, the result was passed to all humanity because he was their representative. Christ, the second Adam, who was the other federal representative in the scheme, remedied the situation through the incarnation and his atoning work on the cross.'[13] The thesis is a fairly technical study of distinctive areas in Smeaton's theology in connection with the work of the Holy Spirit in relation to Adam and Christ. Shillaker's main conclusion is that 'Smeaton provides a coherent theory, which does not contradict the tradition of Reformed theology in which he stands.'[14]

Apart from the fact that no biography of him was ever written, there are probably two main reasons why Smeaton is so little known today. On the one hand, he was not an ecclesiastical politician. He rarely took part in General Assemblies and, indeed, it is hard to find any reference to him in the contemporary Minutes of Assemblies.[15] No doubt an involvement in ecclesiastical politics gives a certain spice to a man's career, and therefore provides appealing material for the biographer. Whether or not that is a good thing is another question. The prominence of the 'ecclesiastical politician' has not been particularly associated with times of revival in the churches. Smeaton, clearly, had no taste for the cut and thrust of Assembly debates, nor ambitions as a 'committee man'. In an obituary notice in *The Scotsman*, it was said that, 'He was not an ecclesiastic in the ordinary acceptation of the term. His interest lay not in presbytery or Assembly polemics, but in gospel preaching and quiet study.'[16]

The second reason for neglect is probably the fact that in the late nineteenth century, generally speaking, the rising generation of divinity students became impatient with the older orthodoxy. The old orthodoxy wasn't exciting enough. What was desired was something new and 'progressive'. Several teachers in theological faculties came under the influence of higher critical theories which had come to prominence on the Continent. Besides this, many Free Church students studied in Continental faculties in the second half of the nineteenth century and came under the influence of the theories then prevalent in Germany and Holland. This had the effect of shifting the position the church had held on the verbal and plenary inspiration of Scripture. It also served to shunt large parts of the church into a spiritual wilderness of a sterile scholarship and a liberal theology. The critical movement tended to fall in with the growing evolutionary views of nature. This brought pressure to de-emphasize or marginalize the supernatural elements of biblical faith. After 1859 the world went after Charles Darwin's theory of evolution with ever-increasing sophistication. This had a profound impact on critical studies in religion. The critics overlaid the biblical history by the evolutionary ideas. It transformed a spiritual religion into a simply social gospel.

Smeaton, though not prominently, was one of the few concerned voices raised against such trends in biblical studies. To many students, however, he was an anachronism. Reveal-ingly, Homer Goddard says of Smeaton's position that, 'The most damaging criticism of Smeaton is that he seldom pre-sents a fresh theological concept or view point. He therefore stirs up little antagonism, being considered by many to be one of the old school'![17] It will be recognized that it was Smeaton's position with which issue is taken, and Goddard simply shows his own bias at this point. In terms of breadth of knowledge and acquaintance with the theological literature of the day, it is doubtful that Smeaton could be matched by any other nineteenth-century theologian. 'It ought not to be over-looked,' said Malcolm Kinnear, with reference to Smeaton's volumes on the atonement, that 'Smeaton's two books were the first comprehensive, scholarly, exegetical analysis of the New Testament teaching on the atonement from a British author in this period, and in thoroughness and detail his work has not been paralleled since in the English language. Smea-ton was a learned man of deep religious insight, and this will not go unnoticed by careful readers of his work.'[18]

We have a glimpse of this in Smeaton's monumental book, *The Doctrine of the Atonement as Taught by Christ Himself* (1871). The 'Appendix of notes and historical eluci-dations' at the end of that volume cannot but convince the reader of his immense learning and rigorous critical interac-tion with the literature of the day.[19] Sadly, since Smeaton's day theological science has been largely dominated in Scot-tish theological faculties by neo-orthodox and modernist views.

There has been an evident tendency in the churches to seek status through scholarship which has often compromised the supernatural and divine elements in the biblical faith. There has also tended to be reliance on man's wit and wisdom, rather than upon the work of the Holy Spirit. Such tendencies have been a snare and even a death wish for the church, because they have tended to produce a man-centred religion which denies the supernatural. Such attitudes, then — in ecclesiastical politics and in worldly scholarship — have arguably had a devastating effect, spiritually speaking, on the church in Scotland and elsewhere in the twentieth century. The deterioration in church life in the West is not unrelated to the nineteenth-century 'watershed' which was constituted by a distinct shift in attitudes towards the inspiration and author- ity of the Scriptures as a divine record of a divine revelation.

George Smeaton was a diffident man as far as church courts were concerned. He did not have a prominent career in church affairs. Rather he devoted himself to his work of preaching and teaching, to which the Lord had called him. His task, as he saw it, was to encourage among the rising generations of ministers a right understanding and handling of the Word of God. The effective denial by so many of received views of the inspiration and inerrancy of Scripture caused him great pain in his later years. He was exercised about the consequences of such defection, not least in terms of depar- ture from historic Calvinism and orthodox, biblical Christian faith.

Though he was not a controversialist by nature, George Smeaton was inevitably drawn into controversies as the Free Church slowly but surely changed its position in the latter part of the nineteenth century, especially in relation to the author- ity and sufficiency of Scripture. There is no doubt that Smea- ton was a man of irenical and gracious spirit. Nevertheless, as occasion demanded he raised his voice against the liberalizing trends of his times. It was said in the obituary notice approved by the Free Church General Assembly of 1889 that, 'He took little part in the business of church courts, and but seldom descended into the arena of controversy; yet he held decided opinions and gave no uncertain sound on the debated questions which from time to time arise in the church.' In assessing his life in the church, it is inevitable that his attitudes towards controversial issues will come to the forefront. It was a period of downgrade from the old orthodoxy. In the light of this, his opinions on such debated issues assume considerable importance, not least in view of his position in a chair of a major theological college of the day.

It is not known what became of Smeaton's papers or books, though apparently most of his considerable library was donated to the New College Library, Edinburgh. At the time of his death there was one surviving son, Oliphant, who had emigrated to New Zealand in 1878 and pursued a career first in teaching and then in journalism and writing. Oliphant Smeaton returned to Scotland and occupied the family home after his mother's death in 1893. Though a prolific writer, the only thing he wrote about his father appears to have been the few pages he contributed to William Knight's *Some Nineteenth-Century Scotsmen*, under the title 'Professor Smeaton and his colleagues'.[20] He had charge of his father's papers, but what became of them is not now known. Apart from two handwritten notebooks, one on Sabbath observance, and the other containing notes on books, surprisingly little Smeaton memorabilia is to be found in New College.

This present biographical work is largely original. There is not an abundance of suitable extant and available material to the prospective biographer. The author is, however, indebted to many individuals for help received in various ways in completing this work. Thanks are expressed to the Committee of the Free Church School in Theology for requesting the author to present a paper on George Smeaton at the 2003 school. That served as a spur to contemplate a fuller biography. Indebtedness is acknowledged to the staff at New College Library, Edinburgh, for willing assistance in so many ways in this project. In addition, the encouragement and work of Evangelical Press in undertaking the publication of this work on Smeaton is deeply appreciated. At a personal level it has been a challenging but stimulating and spiritually edifying experience to put together this short biography of one of the foremost of Reformed theologians.

George Smeaton was a man of God, a faithful minister of the gospel, and an accomplished New Testament scholar. It is fitting that lovers of the truth should have rediscovered his major works in more recent times. He has rested from his labours, but his works follow him. It is the prayer and desire of this writer that this work might belatedly be a fitting tribute to one of the ablest of Scottish divines. The concern in the work has been to bring out not only the salient features of a life lived in the service of the Saviour, but also from his various writings to let him speak to the present generation. It is this author's hope and prayer that this may provide a stimulus today to faithfulness to the Lord in sound theological thinking and practical Christian living. This was Smeaton's own desire in his life's work. There are many lessons for our own witness-bearing to the truth today from the life of such a man of God. We are challenged to follow in his steps, as he followed in Christ's.

Smeaton was not one to be 'carried about with various and strange doctrines'. He was a precious gift of God to the church, 'whose faith follow, considering the end of their conversation. Jesus Christ the same yesterday, and today, and for ever' (Heb. 13:7-8). George Smeaton exemplified the truth: 'It is a good thing that the heart be established with grace' (Heb. 13:9). From the standpoint of the classic Reformed theology, he 'served his own generation by the will of God' (Acts 13:36). His whole desire in his ministry was to serve the Lord. To the Lord alone be the glory.

John W. Keddie
Struan, Isle of Skye
August 2007

1.
Roots

George Smeaton was a
direct descendant of the
famous Thomas
Smeaton, the reformer
who succeeded Andrew
Melville as principal of
Glasgow University in
1580.

1.
Roots

Little is known of George Smeaton's immediate family. One famous relative was John Smeaton (1724-92) who made his name as a civil engineer.[1] John Smeaton was one of the most renowned civil engineers of the eighteenth century. Born and brought up in Austhorpe near Leeds, even as a boy John had made models of fire engines and lathes. He was elected a Fellow of the Royal Society in 1753 and six years later received a gold medal for his paper, 'Experimental enquiry concerning the natural powers of wind and water to turn mills'. He studied canal and harbour systems of Holland in 1754. But of all his works, the most famous was the construction of the fourth Eddystone lighthouse, 1756-59.

John Smeaton

The first two Eddystone lighthouses had been put up by Henry Winstanley. On the second he rather boastfully put the inscription, 'Blow, O winds! Rise, O ocean! Break forth, ye elements, and try my work!' Tragically the elements did just that, and the lighthouse came a cropper (i.e. fell down), with Winstanley inside, in a great gale of November 1703! The third, put up by one John Rudyerd, was destroyed by fire in 1755. It must, therefore, have been with some trepidation that John Smeaton set to the task of building the new lighthouse in Eddystone in 1756. He modelled the lighthouse on the trunk of the oak tree, building it of stone, and constructing the foundation with stones interlocked in a dovetail fashion. Upon Smeaton's lighthouse there were no exaggerated claims. Rather at the foot was chiselled the words: 'Except the Lord build the house, they labour in vain that build it' (Ps. 127:1). On the keystone above the lantern were the words, 'Laus Deo!' (Praise be God!). It was completed in 1759.

Unfortunately, in the 1870s it was clear that the rock on which it was based had begun to crack up and it was decided to take the lighthouse down and put up another on a nearby rock. The lower part, with the interlocking stone could not, however, be demolished, and it still stands as a 'stump' alongside the new lighthouse, a perpetual reminder of what was one of the greatest feats of engineering of the eighteenth (or any other) century. The rest of Smeaton's lighthouse, the upper part, was taken down and rebuilt at Plymouth, where it still stands. No doubt the texts upon it were an expression of the engineer's personal faith in God, in which he was at least followed by his grand-nephew.

John Smeaton, incidentally, was also responsible for the Forth and Clyde Canal (1768-90), and founded the Smeatonian Club in 1771. This was a small club for engineers which merged with the Institute of Civil Engineers in January 1818. John Smeaton was buried in the old parish church at Whitkirk, West Yorks, but he is commemorated by a stone in Westminster Abbey.[2]

John Smeaton's Eddystone lighthouse was taken down and rebuilt at Plymouth (above) as a lasting tribute to a great feat of engineering.

These Smeatons were descended from one Thomas Smeton (or Smeaton, 1536-83). 'My father', said George Smeaton's son, Oliphant, '...was a direct descendant of the famous Thomas Smeaton, the Reformer who succeeded Andrew Melville as principal of Glasgow University in 1580.'[3]

Thomas Smeton was a Scotsman, having been born at Gask, near Perth. He was educated at Perth Grammar School and at St Salvatore's College, St Andrews. Brought up in the Catholic church, he became a Protestant in Geneva in 1571. Apparently he was in Paris during the massacre of St Bartholomew's Day on 24 August 1572. It is said that he only escaped death by taking refuge in the home of the English ambassador, Walsingham. When he returned to England he publicly renounced popery. He settled in Colchester before returning to Scotland in 1577 as minister of Paisley Abbey.

James Melville recognized that Smeton's past experience in the Roman Catholic church well suited him to warn the Scottish nation of the dangers of that system. He says of Smeton in his *Diary*, in the quaint language of the day:

He [Thomas Smeton] being weill acquented with the practizes of papists, namlie, Jesuists, and their deuyces for subuerting the kirk of Scotland, bathe publiclie and privatlie, ceasit nocht to cry and warn ministers and schollars to be diligent vpon ther charges and buiks, to studie the controuersies, and to tak head they neglected nocht the tyme, for ther wald be a strang vnseatt of papists. Also, he was carefull to know the religion and affection of noble men, insinuating him in thair companie, in a wyse and graue manor, and warning tham to be war of euill companie, and nocht to send thair berns to dangerus partes. And, finalie, Mr Andro [Andrew Melville] and he marvelouslie conspyring in purposes and judgments, war the first motioners of an anti-seminarie to be erected in St Andros to the Jesuist seminaries, for the course of theolo-

gie, and cessit never at assemblies and court, till that wark
was begun and sett fordwart. [4]

Thomas Smeton was moderator of the General Assembly in
1579 and again in 1583.[5] Married before 1575, he had issue:
Theophilus, Andrew and Thomas.[6] The latter was the ancestor
of John Smeaton, relative of George Smeaton's father.

It was said of Thomas Smeton that, 'In learning he was far
beyond the generality of his brethren, while his manners were
mild and conciliatory.'[7] What was said by Thomas M'Crie
about him was uncannily applicable to his nineteenth-century
descendent, George Smeaton: 'Smeton was well acquainted
with the learned languages, wrote Latin with great purity, and
had not, like many of his countrymen who had been abroad,
neglected his native tongue, in which he composed with great
propriety. In private life he was distinguished for his retired
and temperate habits; encroaching upon the hours usually
devoted to diet and sleep, that he might devote more time to
his studies. Yet his temper was sweet, and his manners affable
and remote from everything like rusticity or moroseness. His
premature death, soon after he succeeded Melville as principal of the University of Glasgow, was an unspeakable loss to
that seminary.'[8]

2.
Early years

Smeaton's mother had 'in her heart consecrated him to God, and resolved to train him for the work of the ministry'.

2.
Early years

1814 saw Napoleon exiled to Elba and the end of the Napoleonic wars. For those interested in literature, 1814 also saw the publication of Jane Austen's *Mansfield Park*, which still enjoys great popularity among lovers of the English novel. It also saw the birth of George Smeaton on 8 April 1814 in the parish of Hume, just south of Greenlaw amidst the rolling border hills of Berwickshire in the south of Scotland. Smeaton was destined to become one of the foremost theologians and scholars of the Victorian era in Scotland.

George Smeaton was one of five children born to George and Janet Smeaton at Caldside Farm, Hume. Born before George were John (1806), Catherine (1808), and Betty, or Betsy (1810). There was also a younger brother, William (1819). Their father was a farmer at Caldside Farm, which was a couple of miles north of Hume on the road towards Greenlaw. From the farm they had a wonderfully scenic outlook due south to the prominent Hume Castle which overshadowed the school they would have attended. George's father had been brought up in a neighbouring parish of Stitchell. His mother's maiden name was Janet Marshall, a native of Hume. In the first census of 1801, the population of the parish of Hume is given as 415.

It is to be assumed that George Smeaton was brought up in a God-fearing home and that early in his life he confessed his faith in Christ as his Saviour. The family would have adhered to the Stitchell Parish Church. Thomas Smith, in a funeral sermon after Smeaton's death, says that Smeaton had often told him that, 'His pious mother having, contrary to her own expectation and that of others, survived his birth, in her heart consecrated him to God, and resolved to train him for the work of the ministry.'[1]

Thomas Smith, later a colleague of Smeaton's at New College, entered the arts and divinity training in Edinburgh on the same day as Smeaton, attended the same classes for eight sessions, and finished the course on the same day in 1838. Of Smeaton's spiritual experience Smith was to remark, 'As to the particulars of the beginning and early progress of his spiritual life, I know nothing. But I know that it was in his boyhood; while from the tenor of his conversation and his preaching in after years, I have no doubt that his acceptance of Christ and of his salvation was a very definite act.'[2]

George Smeaton was educated first in the local parish school, presumably in Hume. He went up to Edinburgh University for arts and divinity as a fifteen-year-old in 1829. Thomas Smith records that in his first session at Edinburgh University he seemed rather disadvantaged by his country schooling. 'But he soon got over this, and took the position in the estimate both of professors and fellow-students of one of the best scholars in his class.'[3]

These men were students of Thomas Chalmers, professor of divinity in Edinburgh and a leader of the evangelical cause in the Kirk. It was said that young Smeaton was a favourite student of the great man. In those days there were no formal prizes in the theological classes, but in Smeaton's last year a political club which was wound up gave £100 to Dr Chalmers to be given as a prize to the best student of his class. The prize went to George Smeaton.[4] Apparently the young student 'at once laid the sum out in books, securing among other things a complete edition of Migné's *Patristic Library* in seventy folio volumes, a first edition of *Calvini Opera*, a fine copy of *Poli Synopsis*, the famous folio *Erasmus* in five volumes, and other treasures'![5]

There is a reference to George Smeaton in the *Memoir of James Halley*. Halley was a divinity student from Glasgow who had come through to Edinburgh to study for a year under Thomas Chalmers. In a letter to one James Morrison dated December 1836, James Halley speaks of an election which had taken place of six curators for the Edinburgh (University) theological library. 'The law is', says Halley, 'that Dr Chalmers proposes thirty-six from whom the students select six... And, in the vote, the two highest were Smeaton, 81; Halley, 80. Aren't the Edinburgh folks really φιλόξενοι [i.e. hospitable]?'[6] It is quite clear that Smeaton, then in his penultimate year of divinity training in Edinburgh, was a popular student who would have 'known his books'.

In his time at Edinburgh University, Smeaton committed to memory every word in a great folio Greek lexicon! Smith asked him many years later whether this was true, to which he received the answer with a smile: 'Well, there was some truth in it. I suppose you did foolish things yourself in those days.'[7] Whether it was foolish or not, it was clear even at that early stage he was destined to have a commanding knowledge of Greek language and literature. John Macleod reminds us that Smeaton was 'the most eminent scholar of the set of young men who with M'Cheyne and the Bonars sat at the feet of Chalmers'.[8]

In the late 1830s several young ministers organized what they called the 'Exegetical Society'. There is a note written by Robert Murray M'Cheyne in Edinburgh on 24 May 1838, which indicates the purpose of the society: 'We the undersigned members of the Exegetical Society hereby declare our intention to read during the course of next year the books of Isaiah and Jeremiah or one or other of them in Hebrew, and one of the books of the New Testament in Greek.' It is signed by Henry Moncrieff, Andrew A. Bonar, Robert Kinnear, Thomas Brown, Walter Wood, John Thomson, Alexander N. Somerville, George Smeaton, and Robert Murray M'Cheyne. These men were to become influential in the early days of the Free Church following the Disruption of 1843.[9]

Exegetical Society rules with signatures (1838)

In his *Memoir of the Rev. R. M. M'Cheyne*, Andrew Bonar
says of this society: '...No society of this kind (i.e. for fellowship and Bible study) was more useful and pleasant to us than
one which, from its object, received the name 'exegetical'. It
met during the session of the theological classes every Satur-
day morning at half-past six. The study of biblical criticism,
and whatever might cast light on the word of God, was our
aim.' Every meeting was opened and closed with prayer.

Minutes of the discussions were kept; and the essays read were preserved in volumes.[10]

The society demonstrated a commitment the men had to the study of the original languages, which arguably puts more recent generations of divinity students to shame. This linguistic interest no doubt laid the groundwork for the service to which George Smeaton was later called in the Free Church.

After completing his divinity training in Edinburgh, George Smeaton was licensed by the Church of Scotland Presbytery of Edinburgh on 28 March 1838. He was appointed thereafter as missionary, or assistant, in the North Leith Parish, of which the minister was James Buchanan, later to be a colleague in New College.[11]

3.
Preaching

In his understanding of true preaching, Smeaton was clearly in the line of the best traditions of the historic experiential Calvinism of the Scottish Reformed church in its best days.

3.
Preaching

George Smeaton was not long in Leith before being elected to the charge of Morningside in Edinburgh on 31 December 1838. He was ordained and inducted there on 14 March 1839. His stipend was £80 per annum.[1] Morningside at that time was a village to the south-west of the city of Edinburgh.

The original Morningside Parish Church was situated at the corner of Morningside Road and Newbattle Terrace. It was a daughter church of St Cuthbert's in the west end of Edinburgh. The architect was John Henderson and the first services took place on 29 July 1838. The church began its days in the active times of church extension just before the 1843 Disruption. Thomas Chalmers lived in Morningside and was the driving force for the building of the original Morningside Parish. The church cost just over £2000 to build. The original seating was for 760. It had been declared a *quoad sacra* parish — a sort of church extension work — by the General Assembly on 19 May 1838. Sadly, the building was closed for worship in the late 1990s and became part of Napier University.

Smeaton was not long in Morningside. The following year he was presented by Mr Tyndall Bruce to the central Fife Parish of Falkland to where he was translated on 18 September 1840. It was said that the parish had been, like so many others in Scotland, 'blighted by a cold and un-evangelical ministry for a long season'. When this door opened to him, though he had only been a short time at Morningside, he received the encouragement of Thomas Chalmers, a member in his congregation, and other leading ministers to accept the call, and so to Falkland he went. It seems that 'He set himself

Morningside Parish Church, 1838

bravely but quietly to his work, notwithstanding the difficulties which the laxity of discipline under his predecessors, and a general prejudice against distinctively evangelical preaching placed in his way; and God largely owned his faithful labours.'[2]

On 24 November 1840, shortly after he went to Falkland, George Smeaton married Janet Helen Goold. Janet Goold had been born in Edinburgh on 19 January 1814. She was the youngest daughter of the Rev. William Goold (1776-1844), a Reformed Presbyterian (Covenanter) minister in Edinburgh. The bride's father married the couple.

Janet Smeaton's older two sisters, Isabella and Ann, both married Reformed Presbyterian ministers. Her younger brother, William Henry Goold (1815-97), became a Reformed Presbyterian minister and was among the group that entered the Free Church in 1876, of which union he was a prime mover from the Reformed Presbyterian side. He was particularly well known through his editorship of the works of John Owen, reprinted in recent times by the Banner of Truth Trust. Dr Goold was the last moderator of the Reformed Presbyterians (1876) and was the following year moderator of the Free Church General Assembly! He was minister of Martyrs Memorial Reformed Presbyterian Church on George IV Bridge (1840-76).[3] In 1860 he became secretary of the National Bible Society of Scotland. Goold married Margaret Spiers Symington in 1846. She was a daughter of William Symington (1795-1862), Reformed Presbyterian minister and professor in Glasgow, and author of the famous work, *Messiah the Prince, or The Mediatorial Dominion of Jesus Christ* (1839). William and Margaret Goold had nine children, of which one was named after George Smeaton: George Smeaton Goold was born in 1854 and lived until 1940.

George and Janet Smeaton had the first two of their six children while at Falkland. George was born there on 7 September 1841, and Isabella Burrell, named after Mrs Smeaton's mother, was born on the eve of the Disruption, on 23 April 1843. Thomas Smith speaks of three children of the

Smeatons dying in infancy, though we have now no record of these. Smith does say of Smeaton that, 'Again and again he had to gaze with tearful eyes on the empty crib in the nursery, and to listen in vain for the tramp of the little feet that was as music to his ear.'[4] It is assumed that these children were born and lost between the birth of Isabella in Falkland and William Henry Oliphant, who was born in Aberdeen in 1856.

The examples of George Smeaton's sermons that survive show him to have been strongly evangelical and expository in his style. It was said that, 'His preaching set forth the great evangelical doctrines with rare power and unction.' Another testified that, 'His sermons were full of Christian fervour, and were characterized alike by purity of diction and breadth of scholarship.' Thomas Smith said that, 'Though no doubt there would be a gradual maturing of his powers, yet I suspect that the difference betwixt his earlier and his later preaching was less than in most cases. He was no novice when he began to preach. His youthful energy was not the result of unregulated enthusiasm, and did not give place to cold formality. From the first he knew the gospel in its power, and was able to bring to its proclamation a well-stored and severely disciplined mind. With none of the artificial accomplishments of oratory, and with a mind too earnestly occupied with the matter to give a thought to the manner, the young minister of Morningside preached very nearly as did the venerable professor.'[5]

Of his sermons that were put into print, the earliest is one which appeared in the first volume of *The Free Church Pulpit*, published in 1845.[6] The sermon is on Psalm 89:30-33 and is entitled, 'The Lord's jealousy against backsliders consistent with his unchanging love'. In the sermon Smeaton speaks of the reality of indwelling sin, the danger of personal declension, and how the backslider may be restored. The preacher asks about the beginnings of declension in the soul. He says: 'The sin that dwells in us comes on with noiseless step, disarming all suspicion; it may be under the guise of weariness, or suggesting delay in spiritual service, and it is little suspected. Nay, spiritual slumber is accounted sweet. Indwelling sin is of dreadful strength; and if we cannot trace out all its windings and deceitfulness, if it is a friend within to every temptation from without, and wars in every power of the soul with the Most High, is not the most unwary soul most sure to fall?'

What are the signs of declension? Smeaton mentions several: (1) 'You are not in the same earnest effort' as formerly; (2) 'You have ceased to seek the same blessings'; (3) 'Nor do you pursue the same spiritual exercises.' There will be chastening to bear: 'The Lord, who will not be mocked, inflicts fit punishment for every declension, for all distrust of him. Do ye make light of small departures from the Lord, because it is a day of grace? Do ye wink at decays of grace in yourselves, at sloth or unbelief or a defiled conscience, at lukewarmness in prayer or in holy love, as if God winked, at them too? Ye shall suffer loss though ye may be saved so as by fire.'

The words, 'My loving-kindness will I not utterly take from him,' says Smeaton, show us, 'the proper motive to be brought to bear on sad backsliders, and the Lord's way of restoring them'. The backslider is to rest his or her soul upon the Lord alone, for, 'However near we live to God, there is no other way of pleasing God, no other way of coming under the warm beams of the Father's love, than the plea from hour to hour to hour which is founded on his Son.'

Here is the way back from declension: 'Draw not your comfort or your confidence from anything wrought in you as a ground of faith, but look simply to God giving you his Son, and all the fullness of his Son, in the precious promises. Cast yourself on God's self-moving grace without you, and peace will fill your soul, within.'

This is a moving, experiential sermon in the very best traditions of Reformed preaching in Scotland.

Another printed sermon was one on Acts 1:5-8. It is entitled 'A witnessing church — a church baptized with the Holy

Ghost'. This sermon was preached before the Free Synod of Perth on 21 April 1846 and was published at the request of the synod.[7] In the sermon Smeaton challenges his hearers: 'O, if we can sit as a church or as individuals, in easy fellowship with sinners, not seeking to save souls, not daring to encounter the adversary, face to face, we show that we are not baptized with fire!'[8] He goes on to say later: 'If slothful in seeking God in prayer, in cultivating a holy relish for the things of God, if we never pray unless peculiarly helped, if we never put forth any activity in holiness unless God give victorious aid, can we have this fiery baptism?'[9] To the church he challenges: 'A church is only so far a witnessing church as it is thus baptized with the Holy Ghost.'[10] To the preacher he says: 'Can he be a witness of the Lord's abiding with his people to the end of the world, who knows not in his heart a daily intercourse with Jesus — who has not the witness of the Spirit that he is a child of God?'[11] To believers in general he also directs a challenge: 'Nothing, it seems to me, will strike the heart of this callous age, but new holiness in believers' lives — the awe-inspiring spectacle of men glowing with love to their Lord, openly separating from the world.'[12]

Even as early as 1846 Smeaton was sounding a warning concerning the future of the Free Church. 'No church in Christendom', he says, prophetically, 'is more exposed than ours to self-complacency for its sacrifices, its devotedness, its self-denial, more liable to be elated with unexpected success, more prone to glory in its ministers, its means, its numbers, and its contributions, in its schemes, in its prominent position before the world's eye.'[13] He quotes Thomas Hooker on embarking to New England with the Pilgrim fathers, expressing his apprehensions: 'Farewell, England, I expect now no more to see that religious zeal and power of godliness which I have seen among professors in that land. Adversity has slain its thousands, but prosperity its ten thousands. I fear that those who have been zealous Christians in the fire of persecution will become cold in the lap of peace.'[14]

To this Smeaton adds: 'May the Lord keep this Free Church awake at whatever cost!' And he concludes: 'Say not, "O, that a dead world were quickened"; but, "O, that I myself were quickened".'[15]

Ten years later his sermon preached before the Free Synod of Aberdeen was also printed. This time the subject was, 'The real presence of Christ in the midst of his people', on Revelation 2:1, delivered on Tuesday, 8 April 1856 in Aberdeen. Besides the circulation of such sermons, the only other examples of Smeaton's preaching are sermons delivered on the occasion of the passing of friends and colleagues. But these are clear indicators both of his understanding of the nature of preaching and in particular of his delight in gospel preaching.

George Smeaton's concern for his students in relation to preaching is found in an address to divinity students at New College at the close of the college session on 27 April 1872. His subject was, 'The true preacher'. He speaks particularly of the elements that enter into a successful ministry, that is to say, in the highest sense. He first of all mentions some 'obstructions' that stand in the way of a successful ministry, humanly speaking: 'Nothing contributes to render the gospel unfruitful than a system of reserve in setting forth the grand distinctive doctrines of the gospel.'[16] He suggests that this had begun to prevail, something he puts down 'partly to theological bias, and partly to a desire to be on good terms with the spirit of the age'. We are reminded that there is nothing new under the sun. Smeaton reminds us to guard against such a hindrance to effective gospel work. He then suggests that, 'Want of success is sometimes due to this, that Scripture terms are too sparingly used, and appeals to Scripture authority as equivalent to divine authority, are unwarrantably withheld.'[17]

That Smeaton's warning was not entirely heeded is sadly evident from the subsequent history of the Scottish church. The progressive departure from Scripture authority bankrupted much preaching in Scotland in the latter part of the nineteenth and right through the twentieth centuries. A third reason for the blunting of pulpit ministry Smeaton puts down to this: 'a defect in enforcing the obligations of Christian ethics on regenerate men'.[18] By this he means that unless there is rigorous application of the ethical norms of the Word of God in the life, sound doctrine itself will not long survive.

George Smeaton clearly discerned a weakening in the handling of such things as divine judgement and the enormity of the guilt of sin. He ends his address with several pointed words of application:

First, 'Expound the divine word consecutively, and in its connections, as well as preach on separate texts.'[19] It is important, he maintains, that the people see the Word in its connections as it relates to their lives.

Second, 'Familiarize your minds, as students and preachers, with the experience and habits of successful labourers in the vineyard.'[20] Here he mentions John Welsh, George Whitefield, John Bunyan, David Brainerd and Asahel Nettleton as inspiring zeal in those who come after them.

Third, 'Let me add self-examination and prayer.'[21] Here Smeaton quotes the Puritan Thomas Hooker: '"Prayer," said Hooker, the eminent Pilgrim father and pillar of the New England colony, "prayer is the main work of a minister, and that by which he must carry on all the rest."'[22]

All this is perennially relevant for preachers. It comes with as much power and challenge to the church today as it had for those divinity students to whom he first directed his exhortations, for we are in great need of rediscovering just such concerns in the preaching of the unsearchable riches of Christ today.

It is interesting that at an earlier date, in a tract on *The Improvement of a Revival Time* — which we take to have been written at the height of the 1859-60 revivals which swept through Scotland — Smeaton identifies the primacy of the prayers of the people for the effectiveness of preaching. He says:

> Let me revert for a moment to the place which God's people, his remembrancers, occupy in connection with the progress of this GREAT WORK, which causes joy in heaven, and diffuses gladness on earth. Be united in *prayer*, and give the Lord no rest, till greater things are done by his outstretched arm. 'It is of no use to preach', said Nettleton, 'if the people do not pray.' But the prayer which opens Heaven and brings down the SPIRIT, is not that feeble desire which ceases if it must encounter *delay,* or a *trial* of your patience; but that desire which will not go without the answer, and which asks on a scale not lower than God's 'riches in glory by Christ Jesus'. The prayer which breaks through the clouds, and which God owns, is that which grasps the *promise* as if it were the *accomplishment.* 'What things soever ye desire when ye pray, *believe that ye receive them,* and ye shall have them.' (Mark 11:24)[23]

It is clear that George Smeaton had a deep concern for faithful gospel preaching. He consistently stressed that such preaching should be rooted in the divine authority of Scripture and be accompanied by earnest prayer for the work of the Holy Spirit to bring home the Word with power.

In his understanding of true preaching, Smeaton was clearly in the line of the best traditions of the historic, experiential Calvinism of the Scottish Reformed church in its best days. In a comment on the writings of Ralph Erskine, the eighteenth-century Scottish Secession preacher, Smeaton was to say this: 'The federal [covenant] scheme may be termed the concentrated essence of the Calvinistic system. But in the mind of the Bostons and Erskines it was gracefully associated with the freest and most unfettered announcement of the invitations of the gospel.' He goes on to say that, 'In the federal system, which Erskine knows to wield so skilfully, the high doctrines of sovereign, special, efficacious grace on which the federal system rests are found in perfect harmony with the freest proclamation of the invitations of the gospel.'[24]

Later printed sermons preached by Smeaton on the death of colleagues in the ministry are full of instruction on the nature of preaching and contain solemn appeals to his hearers. After the death of his friend Samuel Miller, late minister at Free St Matthew's, Glasgow, Smeaton at one point speaks of the loss of power in the pulpit compared to earlier days. He says: 'The loss of power in the church compared with former days may be traced in a large measure to the fact that there is little appeal to inspired authority. There is a vague substitution of human opinion in place of that which is divine.' So, what is the corrective? 'The Word of God', he adds, 'must be heard authoritatively as from God, and where that is wanting, men are not sufficiently brought into the presence of God, and before the bar of God as sinners. All powerful preaching is run up to the authority of the oracles of God.'[25] He goes even further in warning of the folly of giving an uncertain sound from the pulpit:

> If the pulpit gives an uncertain sound as to the great articles of the ruin and remedy, redemption and regen-eration, the impressions will be superficial, and little fruit will be reaped. In the dim mirror which is held up, the sinner cannot recognize himself, nor be aroused by the appeal 'Thou art the man.' Preachers adapting themselves to the caprices of modern culture are often silent on the claims, extent and spirituality of the divine law, as if men were no longer comforted by them [pos-sibly 'confronted by them'; there seems to be a printing error in the original]. They ignore the vicarious sacrifice and atoning blood of Christ; they put amendment in place of repentance, pious feeling instead of faith upon the Son of God; they substitute Christian sentiment and

culture for conversion to God, as if man were not a fallen being. Amusing the mind by historic pictures or dramatized delineation of character, they abandon the appeal to conscience and no longer strive to bring men before God's tribunal. Not to speak of the want of faithfulness involved in this, such a method shuts the avenue to the heart.[26]

In this sermon Smeaton closes with a warm appeal:

They who have put off the moment of decision to a more convenient season, have to meet that faithful minister of Christ in presence of their Judge. Where will you appear if you are still impenitent? What a thought is this to the self-righteous, the unconverted, the procrastinating hearer! O awake in time, before it is too late! Let the recollection of all that you heard during the ministry that is now over move you to repentance. Accept the great salvation, which it was the business of his life to commend. At that day, that awful day, his sermons and expostulations will be all recalled, and nothing will be forgotten — recalled from the book of God's remembrance, as well as your own memory.[27]

In a sermon after the death of James Begg in 1883, Smeaton stresses in one place the necessary dependence of the preacher upon the Lord in his preaching: 'He proclaims the message of reconciliation, with the greatest power and effect when he is most in the *attitude of dependence* — when he prays with the greatest abasement, when the proclamation of the gospel comes from one who cherishes an entire and absolute dependence on God.'[28]

It was said of Smeaton later that his prayers in classes at New College 'brought the heavens near'. It is clear that this was also a strong feature of his preaching through his life. In the sermon after the death of James Begg, he speaks of the rewards for the saved. Among many beautiful things said, he refers to what he calls the 'beatific vision'. There is an infinite compensation for all that the redeemed of the Lord may have suffered in their lives of service for the Lord. He says:

> The Lord their God, whom they now know only by faith, and in whom they here find much that is still incomprehensible, will then be fully known, for ever beheld, as well as intimately enjoyed. The beatific vision, consisting in the full display of all God's attributes as seen in Christ, who is the image of the invisible God, is a theme of the greatest moment, the discussion of which, when rightly handled, is highly sanctifying... It was a favourite theme with Howe, Baxter, Shepherd and others of the Puritans, whose theology was largely influenced by the study of the divine attributes, and who contemplated the blessedness of the righteous in seeing God.[29]

For all his great learning and scholarship, Smeaton always had a preacher's heart. His few printed sermons are expository and experiential gems. He preached the eternal realities with power, never failing to give out the warmest invitations to sinners to come to Christ.

4.
The Free Church

'Thus in one day *the Free Church of Scotland,* as she fitly called herself, started into vigorous existence. Her very name implied nationality and connexion with the historical Church of Scotland.'

4.
The Free Church

Trained in the school of Thomas Chalmers and David Welsh, George Smeaton had sympathy with the non-intrusionists in the 'Ten Years' Conflict' which lead to the Disruption of the National Church in May 1843.[1] Chalmers (1780-1847), professor of divinity at Edinburgh University, was moderator of the first Free Church General Assembly in May 1843. A man with a prodigious range of talents, he was described by Thomas Carlyle in these terms: 'It is not often that the world has seen men like Thomas Chalmers, nor can the world afford to forget them; or in its careless mood be willing to do it. Probably the time is coming when it will be more apparent than it is now to everyone, that here, intrinsically, was the chief Scottish man of his time.'[2] Chalmers was a theologian and preacher of extraordinary power and an outstanding leader in the church.

David Welsh (1793-1845) was a colleague of Chalmers' in the divinity faculty of Edinburgh University, in which he was professor of ecclesiastical history. Welsh was the moderator of the Church of Scotland Assembly in May 1843 when he laid on the table the 'Claim, Declaration and Protest' against the encroachments of the state into the jurisdiction of the church. With Chalmers he led many hundreds of sympathetic ministers and elders from St Andrew's Church, George Street, Edinburgh, down to the Tanfield Hall, Canonmills, to convene the first General Assembly of the Church of Scotland, Free.

George Smeaton was among over 400 ministers who on Tuesday, 23 May, at Tanfield Hall signed the 'Act of Separation and Deed of Demission' by which they forsook the status and privileges — and emoluments — of ministers of the Church of Scotland. Eventually 481 ministers, together with 21 missionaries and many hundreds of thousands of people, left the established church and formed the Free Church of Scotland.[3]

Picture taken from D. O. Hill's painting of the Disruption, 1843.
George Smeaton is third from the left in the middle row. To the right of
Smeaton are James Buchanan and James Bannerman, future colleagues
in New College.

Smeaton in one place states very clearly what the Disruption involved:

Thus in one day *the Free Church of Scotland*, as she fitly called herself, started into vigorous existence. Her very name implied nationality and connexion with the historical Church of Scotland. She arose, *not as a sectarian de-*

nomination, not as assuming any new ground or principle unknown to the confessors and martyrs of Scotland. She repudiated, and will repudiate, the attitude of *a sect*. She was conscious of being, what she called herself, *the Church of Scotland, Free*, and would not break her connexion with the past three centuries of Scottish church history. The principle of a national establishment of religion as the fitting homage of the nation, and as the duty of the nation to Christ, the Prince of the Kings of the Earth, was her avowed principle, and could not be surrendered by her without becoming a new church and forfeiting her name. Her protest was not against the Establishment as such, but against the submission with which the Establishment succumbed to the usurpations and encroachments of the civil power. And had a protesting minority continued within the pale of the Establishment, maintaining the church's independence and the people's rights, they would have had the warm sympathy of every Free Churchman. The footing on which they resolved to go out, and on which the practical steps were taken with a view to a new organization, was unmistakably put before the public to this effect.[4]

In later years Smeaton was to characterize the Disruption movement in this way: 'The whole movement sprang from a revival of religion — to say nothing more in detail of that remarkable outpouring of the Holy Spirit, which, like a Pentecostal effusion, visited Kilsyth, Dundee, Perth, Strath-Tay, Aberdeen, in the south, and various places all over Ross-shire in the north... That awakening intensified the religious feelings of the community, and prepared tens of thousands for maintaining the testimony for the headship of Christ, in which, but for this, many would have felt little interest.'[5]

He goes on: '...A revival accompanied the Disruption as well as preceded it. Thousands were impressed and awakened to divine things who were indifferent before. The

testimony to Christ as a real Prince and Head awoke many;
the self-denial of the demitting pastors led others to enquiry;
the new message that arrested and solemnized the congregations everywhere, and especially in long shut-up parishes
where moderate doctrine had blinded the eyes of men, were
all-important elements. But above all the Spirit of God
accompanied the Word.'[6]

Smeaton, then, came out of the Church of Scotland at the
Disruption and was instrumental in forming a Free Church
congregation in Falkland. He conducted the first Free Church
communion service there on the West Green on 16 July
1843. The congregation worshipped in the first five months
following the Disruption in the Congregational church building in Falkland. By then Smeaton had received a call to the
emerging Free Church congregation in Auchterarder.

The Free Church at Falkland, however, did not let him go
easily. In the *Minutes* of Auchterarder Free Church we find
this: 'The congregation of Falkland had appeared before
Presbytery and objected to Mr Smeaton's removal... The
committee heard this report and considered the great importance of urging Mr Smeaton's translation to Auchterarder.'[7] At
the Presbytery meeting at Cupar on 22 August 1843, the
Minutes state that, 'The presbytery resolved ... Mr Smeaton
be loosed from his present charge and translated to Auchterarder according to the rules of the church... From which
judgement Mr Brodie dissented on the ground that the
removal of Mr Smeaton will be productive of very great injury
to the cause of Christ at Falkland, while his settlement at
Auchterarder will be of comparatively little advantage.'[8]

'With his accustomed forthrightness and brevity,' says
Homer Goddard, 'Smeaton's move to Auchterarder is signified
in a letter in the files of Auchterarder's St Andrew's Church
written on a scrap of paper: "Rev. Sir: I hereby accept the call
from the congregation at Auchterarder and am your ob't
servant. George Smeaton" (addressed to the moderator of

Auchterarder Presbytery, dated 26 August 1843).'[9] To Auchterarder, therefore, he removed towards the end of 1843.

Auchterarder is a village about thirteen miles south-west of
Perth on the road to Stirling. It was essentially a village of one
long street in the Strathallan valley. Auchterarder will ever
remain notorious in the annals of Scottish church history. It was
there in 1834 that a spark was lit which initiated the Ten Years'
Conflict leading ultimately to the Disruption itself. For it was at
Auchterarder that the first dispute arose over patronage and the
interference of the civil courts which led to conflict within the
national church and with the civil authorities.

A Free Church congregation was formed in Auchterarder
at the Disruption and a call was immediately sent to George
Smeaton at Falkland, signed by 850 souls. The call was duly
accepted, and Smeaton laboured for ten years in that congregation, devoting himself, it is said, 'with unwearied energy to
every part of pastoral duty'.[10] His early ministry there was
undertaken in a 'tent' erected for field preaching, but a
building was begun on 12 November 1843 and completed
with the erection of a tower in 1845. A manse was built in
1850, just behind the church, which was on the High Street in
the village. The church was just a stone's throw from the
Parish Church building. In a way it dominated the village,
with its very striking square tower on which was written
'Jehovah Jireh' ('the Lord will provide'), together with the
date 1845. It was a substantial church building, with a 'horse-
shoe' gallery, and it would accommodate around 900 people.
After 1900, this became known as St Andrew's United Free
Church, but, sadly, in the late twentieth-century the building
went out of use as a church and was taken over as a furniture
showroom and workshop. The original pulpit went to the
Baptist church in Stirling.

At the time of George Smeaton's ministry in Auchterarder
there was a profound spiritual awakening in the district. 'His
ministry in Auchterarder', said one who had attended upon it

Free Church, Auchterarder (taken c. 1912)

in earlier days, 'was one of great spiritual fruitfulness. Many young men and women whom I know owned their souls' life to his instrumentality, and spoke of him as their father in Christ.'[11] It is recorded that in 1848, halfway through his ministry in Auchterarder, the membership of the Free Church congregation in Auchterarder amounted to 770 souls. Such was George Smeaton's missionary verve that a mission work was begun in nearby Aberuthven, a place some miles north-east of Auchterarder on the road to Perth. That particular village was then renowned for hand weaving. A missionary was subsequently appointed and a church was built there in 1851.

In these years the young minister devoted himself to the study of theology amidst his other pastoral and preaching duties. He acquired in the process knowledge of Dutch and German, to add to Latin, Hebrew and Greek with which he was already familiar. It was such personal study that fitted him for the teaching work the church was to call him to take up for the first time in 1853. Smeaton was a man of prayer. He was a faithful gospel preacher. He could say with the apostle Paul: 'I have not shunned to declare to you the whole counsel of God' (Acts 20:27). But he was also clearly a man of diligent and disciplined study. Of his work and ministry it could surely be said that he took heed to himself and to the doctrine, with the consequent fruit of blessed congregations and students (1 Tim. 4:16).

5.
Aberdeen

'If there is one principle
more important in my eyes
than any other ... as a
moving spring of action in
the minds of the rising
ministry, it is just the
highest cultivation of the
spiritual life, in
combination with the
highest appreciation of
orthodox doctrine.'

5.
Aberdeen

In a rare note about his father, Oliphant Smeaton says that a few months before the Disruption, his father had been approached about expected vacancies in the theological faculties in Glasgow and Edinburgh and whether he would accept nomination for either of them. To such approaches George Smeaton replied: 'While profoundly sensible of the high honour thus paid me, I trust I shall not be thought ungrateful if I say that I could accept nothing, until the present anxious crisis in the church has passed.'[1]

It was not long, however, before the Free Church was to call on his services in the area of the theological education of its students. Though it was felt from the beginnings of the Free Church in 1843 that some provision for theological education ought to be made in Glasgow and Aberdeen, the matter of having separate colleges in these cities was a highly controversial one in the church, and for many years up to 1853 raised the temperature in General Assemblies. William Cunningham (1805-61), principal and professor of church history at New College, Edinburgh, felt that the erection of colleges outside the one in Edinburgh would lead to variations in the quality and content of the theological education, as it was not feasible — as he saw it — to cover all the subjects adequately in Glasgow or Aberdeen, and it would simply multiply costs and resources unnecessarily, besides increasing the danger of heresy.

In that connection it is of more than passing interest that subsequent problems with William Robertson Smith and A. B. Bruce arose from within the Aberdeen and Glasgow Colleges. On this issue there was a falling out between Cunningham and R. S. Candlish. Candlish (1806-73) was a leading Free

Churchman, and as minister of Free St George's in Edinburgh was considered one of the foremost evangelical preachers of the day. The view of Candlish and others, including James Begg at that time, eventually prevailed, and, given the necessary endowments, a fully-fledged college was established in 1854, at which point divinity students would spend only one year at Edinburgh, rather than the two previously required.

Prior to this, Alexander Black had been appointed a theological tutor in 1843 before being moved the following year to Edinburgh as professor of exegetical theology. In 1845, James Maclagan (1788-1852) was appointed theological tutor in Aberdeen. After he died in 1852, the General Assembly the next year decided to appoint Patrick Fairbairn (1805-74) as tutor in theology with George Smeaton as his assistant.[2] Smeaton had become highly regarded as a capable scholar and theologian. He had acquitted himself well in his university course, and had been singled out as a keen and able student in the field of Greek and New Testament language and literature.

In 1853, George Smeaton was called by the church to take up the work of a tutor in theology in Aberdeen as assistant to Patrick Fairbairn. His lectures in systematic theology were to students of the second and third years. He accomplished this while retaining his charge in Auchterarder. In his introductory lecture delivered on 9 November 1853, Smeaton sets out very clearly what he sees as of primary importance in training for the ministry: 'If there is one principle more important in my eyes than any other, or one which I am more peculiarly anxious to place, or to see placed, as a moving spring of action in the minds of the rising ministry, *it is just the highest cultivation of the spiritual life, in combination with the highest appreciation of orthodox doctrine*. And these principles must be lived before they can be taught.'[3]

As if to emphasize this principle, Smeaton goes on to say: 'It is impossible to be too eager in the advancement of the spiritual life, on the one hand; and it is impossible to cultivate too ardently that holy doctrine, the study of which properly

arises from the spiritual life, and which tends to nourish and
to invigorate that life in all its parts.'[4]

Smeaton is concerned that there be consistency between
doctrine and life. 'Theology is not all doctrine', he says.
'Man's nature is not all intellect. He is heart as well as head;
and, while we plead for orthodoxy with all earnestness, we
mean living orthodoxy, or truth embosomed in the spiritual
life. Dead orthodoxy', he goes on to say, 'is a tendency as
calamitous, and a spectacle as painful, as that against which
we have sought to erect a beacon of warning. The intellectual
must not predominate to the exclusion of the spiritual. Dogma
and life must be one organic whole, and be placed in perfect
harmony. Christianity is not a mere system of opinions, but a
renewing power to pervade the whole faculties from the
inmost centre of man's being. It is not a mere doctrine, but a
divine life, destined to transform humanity.'[5] There is every
reason to believe that this was a principle Smeaton held to
consistently throughout his college teaching days. To his
students Smeaton made the following practical appeal:

> One word in conclusion. Endeavour to keep up the
> freshness of spiritual impressions on your own minds
> while engaged in the ardent and strenuous study of
> theology. I need say nothing to convince you that the-
> ology is the noblest study under heaven. I need say
> nothing to convince you that, in this high walk, the
> whole faculties receive the noblest consecration of
> which they are susceptible. But I may add a warning. It
> must not be concealed that students of divinity, more
> than almost any other class, run the risk of growing ir-
> reverently familiar with solemn truths. They are too apt,
> from the circumstance that they are professionally con-
> nected with the daily discussion of sacred truths, to
> grow common-hackneyed in a round of thought about
> the truth. Many grow seared and secular, cold and
> withered, in their personal religion. Avoid this with the

utmost vigilance. Live upon the truth you study; and, the more you live upon the truth, the more vividly will you comprehend it. The more close you walk with God, the more full and unclouded will be your understanding of divine things.[6]

At least the Free Church divinity students who came under the teaching of Smeaton were left in no doubt as to the basis for a sound and spiritual ministry. As one reflects on the history of the Free Church in the second half of the nineteenth-century, it seems undeniable that the ministry of the church in general tended to lose this vision and balance and become preoccupied with the intellect over the heart. The experiential Calvinism stressed by teachers like Smeaton sadly tended increasingly to become marginalized in the Free Church, to its great impoverishment.

Fairbairn and Smeaton were appointed professors, respectively, of theology and New Testament exegesis, at the 1854 Assembly when the status of the Aberdeen College was finally settled. By that time, as we have stated, endowments received were sufficient to raise Fairbairn and Smeaton to full professorships. In the 1854 General Assembly, Smeaton's name was put forward for the second Chair in Aberdeen as the unanimous nomination of the college committee. The Rev. Robert S. Candlish moved the appointment. Candlish speaks of Smeaton's faithful labours as an 'indefatigable pastor'. He goes on to say that 'It is also well known that he is one of those who, in the retirement of his country manse, has been not only keeping up those literary attainments which he acquired at college, but has been steadily and enthusiastically pursuing his studies, till, I believe, it may be said of him at this hour, that he is one of the most accomplished and best theologians we have [applause].'[7] The motion was unanimously agreed to, a notice of this was sent to Smeaton at Auchterarder, and his letter of acceptance was received by the Assembly on 26 May.

How did Smeaton react to this new position as a college professor? In his introductory lecture at the Aberdeen Divinity Hall on 7 November 1854, he took as his subject 'The basis of Christian doctrine in divine fact'. At the beginning of the lecture he makes some comments that beautifully express his feelings:

...In entering today on a new stadium of life, at the margin of which one looks before and behind, the blended recollections of the past and anticipations of the future fill my mind with very mingled emotions. One stadium lies behind me — that of my ministry, which of all scenes in my memory, is the most fresh and fragrant. As to the future, its form and fashion are unknown. But a happier period than has been passed in the ministry of the word I can never hope to enjoy in this world. Nothing could compensate, indeed, to a professor for the loss of the pastoral relation, or could prompt him to resign it, if the office with which he is invested did not, in a manner, lead him to minister to the church at large, and prove serviceable to others who are to occupy that relation which he himself has felt to be so blessed. Were there no prospect of this sort, his cold literary labour would be a poor exchange. But the ulterior prospect of contributing, by the blessing from on high, to form and equip a ministry who shall, in their day, acquit themselves as a good savour of Christ, reconciles me to forego a relation, which, in proportion as it is sustained on both sides by spiritual communion, forms the fairest and most pleasant oasis in this world. He who holds the stars in his right hand, appointing to each his place, seems, moreover, to have indicated, with sufficient clearness, through the church, his will and my duty; and he may have service for me in this place, in company with my colleagues, with whom it is a privilege to be associated. I have loved the preaching of the Word above every other occupation.

But if enabled to communicate to the rising ministry the disposition to regard their work, in any sphere, as the highest, happiest, and noblest on earth; if a band of Brainerds, Neffs, M'Cheynes, rise up around us; if we behold coming forward to supply the ministerial ranks men of faith, zeal and prayer, whose joy in their work shall find expression in the words of Rutherford, 'Next to Christ I have but one joy: the apple of the eye of my delight is to preach Christ my Lord', then I shall feel that the pastoral relation, with its sunny confidence and fragrant ordinances, has not been resigned in vain.[8]

This was the beginning of an eminent service Smeaton gave to the church in the field of theological teaching. In his time in Aberdeen he attached himself to the West Free Church, then under the excellent ministry of Alexander Dyce Davidson (1807-72). Davidson, it was said, was 'one of the best preachers of a day that saw many famous preachers'.[9] Smeaton became an elder in the congregation. In Aberdeen a son, William Henry Oliphant, was born to the Smeatons on 24 October 1856.

After just four years at Aberdeen, upon the retirement of Alexander Black (1789-1864) from the Chair of New Testament exegesis in New College, Edinburgh, in 1856, George Smeaton was elected and appointed to that Chair, taking up his duties in 1857. Black, incidentally, was a man of considerable learning. It was said in W. Ewing's *Annals of the Free Church of Scotland* (1914) that he could converse in nineteen languages and correspond in twelve![10] Apparently so highly was Smeaton's work in Aberdeen valued that when the proposal was made to remove him to Edinburgh, a petition was drawn up in Aberdeen and signed by over 500 ministers, office-bearers and members of the church, in addition to the students, 'praying him to remain in the "Granite City"'.[11] In the event it was, however, of no avail. To Edinburgh he was called, and to Edinburgh he would go.

6.
New College, Edinburgh

...George Smeaton's
attitude to his teaching
work always had a positive
concern for the promotion
of the gospel through men
properly grounded in the
truth.

6.
New College, Edinburgh

When the need for a replacement for Alexander Black as professor of New Testament exegesis at New College, Edinburgh, came up in the 1857 General Assembly, several names were put forward. R. S. Candlish, who had supported Smeaton's appointment to the Aberdeen Chair in 1854, this time moved the name of Robert Rainy (1826-1906), then minister of the Free High Church, Edinburgh. Other names moved were those of David Brown (Glasgow) and Alexander S. Paterson (Glasgow). In addition, George Smeaton's name was put forward by the Rev. William Cousin (Irvine)[1] whose opening remarks were: 'I am quite sure I have only to mention the name of Professor Smeaton of Aberdeen — (hear, hear) — to draw forth a unanimous feeling of respect for him.' In the course of his recommendation of Smeaton, Cousin rather cleverly quoted at length from the recorded speech of Candlish's in favour of Smeaton in 1854!

Cousin's seconder was John Edmonston (1801-65), a Disruption minister who ministered in Ashkirk in the Borders and who assisted in the production of the *Works* of John Owen. Edmonston's speech was a mixture of humour and the utmost seriousness. He began by saying that Smeaton 'had … the best certificate that was ever given a candidate for a professorial chair in that House', as they had just heard from William Cousin's quotation from Candlish's 1854 speech. He went on to suggest that after all Rainy's specific qualifications for the Chair were somewhat thin, able as he undoubtedly was. 'It was no recommendation, and went for nothing, that a candidate for the exegetical Chair was possessed of these ordinary attainments.' What was required then? 'Was it enough to say that a man aspiring to this office had the ancient languages?' No, it was not enough. He needed more than the acquaintance with them acquired through high school, academy or college: 'He must ... not only ... know Hebrew, Chaldee, Syriac, and several other languages with whose barbaric names he would not disturb the ears of the Assembly, but he ought to be intimately acquainted with the Hebrew Scriptures, and familiar with the Septuagint version ... in order to supply the science of exegesis to the New Testament.' He went on to say: 'As for the Greek Testament itself, he ought to be able to take it in his hand and read it off fluently in English. He must also be able, not at second-hand, but for himself, to make use of the Syriac, and other ancient versions for determining many nice points as to the true reading of the original text, and in many cases, also, the true rendering. Unless possessed of these' — we wait for this with bated breath! — 'and other peculiar qualifications which he shortly enumerated, he could not vote for any man as a fit person to fill an exegetical Chair.'[2] The fact that he supported the appointment of George Smeaton speaks volumes of his regard for that man's linguistic attainments.

When the vote came, first of all there was a division between Smeaton and Rainy, which went in favour of the former by 203 votes to 119. Paterson having withdrawn, the final vote was between Smeaton and Brown, in which the vote for Smeaton was 181 against Brown's 163. Accordingly George Smeaton was declared elected to the Chair of exegetical theology, 'amid loud applause'.[3] He communicated his acceptance of the position to the Assembly on 28 May[4] and gave the introductory lecture at the college later that year, on Tuesday, 3 November.

At New College, Smeaton became part of an outstanding Senatus which consisted of William Cunningham (1805-61), the principal and professor of church history, James Buchanan (1804-70), the professor of systematic theology, James Bannerman (1807-68), the professor of apologetics and pastoral theology, and the saintly John Duncan (1796-1870), the professor of Hebrew and Old Testament. With the addition of Smeaton, this comprised, from the standpoint of the orthodox Reformed faith, a Senatus of exceptional quality. Writings of these men have been widely reproduced ever since their passing from their labours on earth.

New College Senatus, c. 1860. Back row (left to right): James Bannerman, George Smeaton. Front row (left to right): James Buchanan, William Cunningham, John Duncan.

Of the principal, William Cunningham, Smeaton wrote, 'Cunningham still towers in memory over them all, as in truth, next to Chalmers the representative man of the Free Church… As a scholar he had no rival in his own branch of learning; as an ecclesiastical statesman, he was, after Chalmers, the most sagacious the Free Church has known; as a debater he was perhaps the most convincing and powerful of his day... He must be ranked as one of the very greatest of Scots ecclesiastics.'⁵ Oliphant Smeaton was to write that 'With Dr Buchanan in particular my father had maintained very close relations', and his father besides was a fellow-elder in Chalmers Memorial Free Church, Grange, with Dr Duncan, up to the latter's death in 1870. He was chief mourner at Dr Duncan's funeral.

Smeaton, therefore, took up the teaching of New Testament exegesis at New College in the autumn of 1857. In his first year there was a quinquennial visitation to the college,⁶ and although he had not fully settled in to his course he made it clear what the basic features of his courses would be. The divinity course covered four years. Students would have two years with Smeaton — a junior and a senior class. In the classes four main areas would be addressed: 1) introduction to the New Testament, including questions of the canon; 2) principles of hermeneutics in which the basic text would be that of Johann August Ernesti (1707-81), *Principles of Biblical Interpretation*, translated from the *Institutio Interpretis* by Charles H. Terrot and printed in two volumes by Thomas Clark in 1843; 3) exegetical study of the Gospels, including a view to the synoptic questions and commentary proper; 4) regular commentary on one or other of the Epistles, with constant reference to the Acts of the Apostles as a historical basis.⁷

Smeaton more or less adhered to this format throughout his thirty-two years of teaching. Generally speaking he was engaged for two hours every day teaching a junior and a senior class in New Testament, five days a week. Another hour was often found necessary to hear prescribed discourses from students. The full divinity course covered four years at that period. The course in exegetical theology extended to two years, with the students of the third year taking the junior class, and students of the fourth year taking the senior class. There was one day each week set apart for a review of lectures in which three or four students each time would be

PLAYFAIR'S PLAN. NEW COLLEGE

The plans for New College, Edinburgh. The building was opened in 1850.
George Smeaton was a professor there from 1857 until his death in 1889.

'Presbyterian Ridge' at the top of the Mound in
Edinburgh, dominated by the New College building

examined. A monthly essay was expected from every student of the senior class. When asked on one occasion whether the church might do anything to improve the efficiency of his work, Smeaton answered that he felt that the most desirable thing was a longer session, or, preferably, a summer session.

In an article contributed to *The British and Foreign Evangelical Review* in January 1862, Smeaton makes reference to the task of exegetical theology which provides an insight into his general approach to his discipline: 'The task of reproducing apostolic doctrine, and of putting it together in its organic connections, is daily becoming a more urgent duty. And the part assigned to exegetical theology is to recall, as far as may be, not only single phrases, but the general outline of those fresh times when apostles, as the chosen organs of Christ's revelation, exhibited in the church the riches of divine grace, as it was discerned by them in the company of the Incarnate Word, and after his ascension.'[8]

That Smeaton's concern in his teaching was not only an academic one, but for an all-round ministry, is evident in a comment he made in answer to a question raised in the quinquennial visitation of 1863 when he commented, 'If I were to name the chief defect in our arrangements in the New College, it is the want of homiletic exercises and pastoral theology which have not been assigned to any of the Chairs.'[9] In the same quinquennial visitation, Smeaton expressed the wish that his students should commit to memory entire books of the Bible!

In those days the remuneration of the professors was about twice the amount of the ministers' stipends. The professors, however, were required to purchase their own homes, whereas ministers occupied church manses. Relatively speaking, the stipends were well up the scale of professional salaries for those days. In Smeaton's case it appears that because the college fund from which professors of all the colleges were paid had been deficient, he did not have parity with the other New College professors for seven years. It was reported to the

General Assembly of 1864 that, 'The salary of Professor Smeaton is now equal to that of his colleagues in the New College.'[10]

No doubt as time went on, George Smeaton would have
occasion to address developing trends, for he did keep
himself abreast of the literature. In his last statement at a
quinquennial visitation, in 1885, he was to say this: 'My
object is to keep my classes as much as possible acquainted
with the true interpretation of the New Testament Scriptures,
and abreast of the best literature on the subject, and to aid
them in forming a proper estimate of its value.'[11]

It may be safely assumed, of course, that his view of the
canon and text of Scripture and its interpretation were soundly
conservative and evangelical throughout. This is perfectly clear
from his own volumes on the atonement and the Holy Spirit,
which are models of sound exegetical theology.

As time went on, sadly, the climate of opinion in the Free
Church shifted from the original solid conservatism and Puritan-
ism to a broader and more liberal perspective. It goes without
saying that reactions of students to classes such as those of 'old
school' men like Smeaton were not sympathetic. 'From the
1870s,' says Kenneth Ross, 'students for the ministry had little
interest in mastering the Calvinist theology which the earlier
professors had taught so thoroughly and fervently. George
Smeaton, the one survivor of the old school in the New College,
did not now capture the sympathy of the students.'[12]

This trend is highlighted in William Robertson Nicoll's biography of the Rev. John Watson, who doubled as a minister
and a novel-writer, the latter under the popular pseudonym of
'Ian Maclaren'. Watson began his course at New College in
1869. Nicoll says this: 'The determined orthodoxy of the Free
Church was beginning to yield. The new generation of
students were eagerly discussing biblical criticism, evolution,
Hegelianism. These acted as solvents on traditional views of
the Bible and on current Calvinistic theology. Watson was
caught in the newer theological movement.'[13]

Watson is typical of the loosening of the old orthodoxy,
something that George Smeaton earnestly lamented. Smeaton, incidentally, would have known Watson well, as he
attended the same congregation at the Grange while a
student at New College.

Even the most impatient of the students, however, had to
acknowledge Professor Smeaton's abilities in his field. There
is an illuminating comment in Norman C. Macfarlane's
biography of the Rev. Donald John Martin. Both Martin and
Macfarlane were students under Smeaton at different times.
This is what Macfarlane says about Smeaton: 'Dr George
Smeaton was a scholarly devout soul, whose earnest prayers
in the class brought the heavens near. He knew his subject,
New Testament exegesis, thoroughly. His students would
have prized the slightest suggestion of heresy such as they
found in his successor [Dr Marcus Dods]. But Dr Smeaton
held on like a full moon slicing its way through the clouds. His
lectures were like golden paths which his students found richly
monotonous... Dr Smeaton never marched his men into the
land of surprises. His son, the late Mr Oliphant Smeaton, used
to say, "My father was not a great but he was a pre-eminently
good man."'[14]

Among Smeaton's earlier students was the Rev. John
George Cunningham (1835-1907), successor to Alexander
Moody Stuart at Free St Luke's in Edinburgh in 1876. Cunningham's attitude was noticeably different from the later
generation of New College students: 'We well remember the
zeal and hope with which the students of our day welcomed
the new professor, and entered eagerly under his able guidance on the exegesis of the New Testament, a department of
theological research which had then only begun to be valued
and cultivated as it deserved. For our own part we found in
the work of the class and in the sympathetic fellowship of the
professor an intellectual impulse and a spiritual impression of
the most helpful and useful kind.'[15] Clearly George Smeaton's
attitude to his teaching work always had a positive concern

for the promotion of the gospel through men properly grounded in the truth.

In those days the college session began on the first Wednesday in November. One of the professors was appointed to give an opening public lecture. The records are now incomplete, but there are reports of Professor Smeaton giving the introductory lectures in 1861 ('Christian ethics and the place that must be assigned them'), 1876 ('On inspiration'), and 1884 ('Retrospect: theological tendencies, discussions and schools of religious opinions of the past fifty years').[16] It is clear that Smeaton was not reticent in addressing theological dangers to be faced and countered by the rising generation of students. No doubt many appreciated this deeply, though all too many, sadly, were ready to go along with the theologically liberalizing flow of the day.

For his contributions to theological education, George Smeaton had been given an honorary doctorate in divinity by Edinburgh University in 1869. This was received from the hand of the chancellor of the university, the Right Honourable John Inglis, the Lord Justice General, at a graduation ceremony held at the university on Wednesday, 21 April. In inviting the chancellor to confer the degree, Thomas J. Crawford, the dean of the Faculty of Divinity said this: 'I have great satisfaction of now presenting to your Lordship the Rev. George Smeaton [applause], professor of exegetical theology in the Free Church College, Edinburgh, who, when prosecuting his studies at this university obtained, in almost every department of learning, the highest academic distinctions; who has for many years discharged with much efficiency the duties of that honourable and arduous office which he now holds; and who, by his numerous theological writings, especially his admirable treatise on the atonement, has greatly contributed to the interest of Christian truth, and established a claim which cannot be gainsaid to the honorary degree of doctor of divinity. [Applause].[17]

In 1874, after the passing of the New College principal, Robert S. Candlish, in 1873, there was a move on the part of some to nominate Smeaton for the principalship of the college. This, however, was not something Smeaton felt himself prepared to take on.[18]

The tide of course was against him, and there was no clearer indication of this than in the appointment of Dr Marcus Dods as his successor in 1889. Dods was of a totally different outlook, and took the Free Church further along the line of a broad and liberal understanding of the New Testament Scriptures which showed little regard for the plenary and verbal inspiration of the documents. It was probably for this reason that Smeaton did not retire from the Chair even when he reached his seventies. In that connection he said in his very last letter: 'I reached my seventy-fifth birthday last Monday. I have had a long and happy life, for which I cannot be sufficiently thankful, and would like now to live for the day. I finished another college session a fortnight ago, and I am just leaving it in the hand of the great Disposer to indicate when I am to stop my public duties. This is a matter on which man cannot direct me. But I know in whose hand I am, and in whose hand are my times.'[19] Little did he think that within a few hours of penning that letter the Master would call him to his eternal rest. Consistent good health and the retention of his basic faculties had enabled Smeaton to complete thirty-two years in the work at New College.

7.
Church affairs

'If the church's mission is
to conquer the world for
Christ, it follows that
believers at home can
never permit themselves to
have a loose connection
with these outposts till the
victory is won — till the
world's mutiny ceases...'

7.
Church affairs

George Smeaton was not a controversialist, or at least we might say that he was a reluctant controversialist. He was not a prominent figure in church courts. Rarely did he speak at General Assemblies. Indeed, rarely did he turn up and take part in General Assembles when he was entitled to do so. A search through the records indicates that of the eleven General Assemblies he might have attended between 1854 and 1885, he only took part in four! Given the professor's decided views on the critical issues of the day, it is sad that his involvement in the church courts was so limited. Towards the end of the Union Controversy — in the late sixties and early seventies — his participation even in college senate meetings noticeably diminished. This is not surprising, since most of his professorial colleagues were pro-union men.

As far as committees were concerned, the only church committee of which he was convener was the committee for the conversion of the Jews (1858-60). Even here he gave up the convenership when he felt it interfered with the effective discharge of the professorate. He did present the report of the committee on the conversion of the Jews in 1859 in one of only two occasions in which he addressed the Assembly. The minutes state that, 'Professor Smeaton, who was received with loud applause, gave in and read the report of the committee for the conversion of the Jews...'[1]

As to the report itself, for which presumably Smeaton was largely responsible, there is a wonderful conclusion which is worth repeating here: 'If the church's mission is to conquer the world for Christ, it follows that believers at home can never permit themselves to have a loose connection with these outposts till the victory is won — till the world's mutiny ceases, and Jew and Gentile lay down their weapons of rebellion. The work is not done when the church sends out her agents, expecting all to go on mechanically. It is done only when the church at home, as becomes the Lord's remembrancers, give him no rest, and never keep silence, imbibing the spirit of Paul, and saying, "My heart's desire and prayer to God for Israel is that they may be saved."'[2]

In the late 1850s there was a widespread experience of revival in the Presbyterian churches in Scotland and Ulster. Around that time Smeaton wrote a 'New Year's tract' on *The Improvement of a Revival Time*. He was particularly concerned to bring out the varied responsibilities of individuals and churches at such a time when, 'In our day, as we hear from one place after another, a mighty power is breaking forth from the kingdom of God, sweeping over the community, bringing salvation to some, and imposing awe on others.'[3] Smeaton is convinced that, 'Beyond all question, Christ is coming in the power of his kingdom.'[4] He ends his tract with powerful and moving words: 'Disciples of Christ have to wait in the youthfulness of simple hope, not for a spirit which they have not, but for more of the spirit which they have. And let us, in order to testify of Christ aright, seek to be daily renewed in the spirit of our mind. Who can testify of the cross, if he does not daily stand fast in the liberty which it brings? Who can tell of Christ's abiding presence with his people, if he does not daily abide in communion with him, and in the enjoyment of his presence? Who can tell of the love of God, if he does not realize that God loves us as he loves his Son (John 17:23) — living under the present sense of an actual and full salvation? But if you do so live, then out of the abundance of the heart your mouth will speak. You will speak because you believe; and weary with forbearing, you will not be able to stay (Jer. 20:9).'[5]

In another place he speaks of the experiences of that revival time: 'Times these are, which prove like another Pentecost, that Jesus lives to dispense the Spirit; when breathless assemblies are hushed in a death-like stillness before the felt presence of the Lord, or the silence is only broken by an irrepressible sigh for mercy. Multitudes of men are looking on with mingled awe and wonder, or with an interest still more personal, while a mighty power, of which they can neither tell the laws nor estimate the force, is breaking forth from the kingdom of God and sweeping over the community. And while the arrows of the King pierce many hearts, a wide-spread fear prevails lest others should be taken and they left.'[6]

Such revival experiences as he enjoyed at Auchterarder in Disruption times, and later in the revivals of 1859-60, made a deep impression on Smeaton's life. They were clearly an important factor in the constancy of his evangelicalism throughout his life, and of his understanding of the works of the Holy Spirit in the world.

Though Smeaton did not enter much into the life of the church courts, his concern for mission was evident throughout, whether in connection with foreign or home missions. The students at New College had a Missionary Society which engaged in mission work in the city, especially in areas of central Edinburgh where the need for such work was so great. In 1861 the Society passed a resolution committing itself to 'missionary operations on an independent footing in some necessitous district of the city', and that 'Professor Smeaton be requested to lend his aid in the undertaking'.[7]

About this time — in 1863 to be precise — the Smeatons came to live in the south side, at 13 Mansionhouse Road (later number 37) in the Grange area of the city, a developing leafy suburb of Edinburgh. There he and other Free Church friends living in that area had a vision for the planting of a church. The nearest Free Churches were at Newington, where his friend James Begg was minister, and, in a westerly direction, Barclay. In point of fact some Free Church folk from

Smeaton residence, 13 Mansionhouse Road, Edinburgh

Roxburgh Free Church, then located in Hill Square, had begun meeting in Clare Hall, on Causewayside, in 1861. This was not too far away. But the Grange folk began services of worship in the dining room at 13 Mansionhouse Road in November 1863. Smeaton also held a prayer meeting in his house. In a letter written on 15 December 1863 to one John Cunningham of 50 Queen Street, Smeaton excused himself from another meeting to which he was invited for this reason: 'I have a prayer meeting in my house every Friday evening.'[8] As far as the service on the Lord's day was concerned, by the third week there were too many for the Smeaton house to hold, and they decided to join up with the worshippers in Clare Hall under the leadership of Professor Smeaton.

The group became so considerable that in 1865 the Presbytery of Edinburgh recognized it as a congregation. A Kirk Session was elected and Professor Smeaton was appointed interim moderator.[9] A building was commenced at the corner of Grange Road and Chalmers' Crescent, and the church was opened on 6 December 1866. It was called the Chalmers' Memorial Free Church, Grange, and is the building now known as St Catherine's in Grange (Church of Scotland).[10] Meanwhile its first minister had been called and inducted. That was Horatius Bonar (1808-89), whose induction took place at Clare Hall on 10 June 1866. For his services in steering the congregation to that point, George Smeaton was presented by them with a silver coffee pot, cake basket and salver, as a mark of their appreciation. Smeaton himself, along with other worthy divines such as John Duncan and William Nixon, became an elder of the congregation until changes brought in to the worship of the congregation took him out of the eldership there and led him to a different congregational affiliation, as explained elsewhere.

Chalmers' Memorial Free Church, Grange (now St Catherine's in Grange). George Smeaton was instrumental in establishing the congregation in 1863 and initiating the church building work.

8.
Union controversy

'Pray that the church may take no step which shall directly or indirectly prove a denial of her Lord, ... that she may not be unfaithful to her past testimony to Christ's special atonement and headship over nations...'

8.
Union controversy

Though not by nature a controversialist, George Smeaton did
not flinch when controversial issues arose. John Macleod says
of Smeaton that he was 'far from being an ecclesiastic in the
ordinary sense of the word, yet he took a deep interest in the
subject of national Christianity'.[1] Barely twenty years had
passed since the Disruption when the Free Church was con-
sumed by an issue which threatened to tear the church in
pieces. This concerned a proposed union with another mainline
Scottish Presbyterian denomination, the United Presbyterian
Church. The United Presbyterian Church had arisen in 1847
from a union of two Secession groups — the 'Relief Church'
and the United Associate Synod of the Secession Church.
These Secession groups had all arisen from splits from the
Church of Scotland the previous century.

A distinctive tenet of the United Presbyterian Church was
what was known as 'voluntarism'. Voluntarism was the theory
in church/state relations that, 'It is not competent to the civil
magistrate to give legislative sanction to any creed in the way
of setting up a civil establishment of religion, nor is it within
his province to provide for the expense of the ministrations of
religion out of the national resources.'[2] State aid, therefore,
was to be excluded in supporting churches, which required to
be maintained only by free-will offerings. In their view it was
unacceptable for the State to exercise its authority and
influence on behalf of religion in any form. It denied the
rightness of the establishment in the nation of true Christian
religion and the support of it by the state authorities.

This was not the position of the Free Church, which very
distinctly maintained the opposite theory, namely, the Estab-

lishment Principle, or, in other words, the responsibility of the state authorities to maintain true Christian faith. In relation to aid given by the State to support the cause of Christ, the Free Church position was as follows: 'As an act of national homage to Christ, the civil magistrate ought, when necessary and expedient, to afford aid from the national resources to the cause of Christ, provided always that in doing so, while reserving full control over his own gift, he abstain from all authoritative interference in the internal government of the church. But it must always be a question to be judged according to times and circumstances, whether or not such aid ought to be given by the civil magistrate, as well as whether or not it ought to be accepted; and the question must, in every instance, be decided by each of the two parties judging for itself, on its own responsibility.'[3]

Thomas Chalmers was very clear on this in his opening address to the first Free Church Assembly on 1843: '...We hold that every part and every function of a commonwealth should be leavened with Christianity, and that every functionary, from the highest to the lowest, should, in their respective spheres, do all that in them lies to countenance and uphold it. That is to say, though we quit the Establishment, we go out on the Establishment Principle — we quit a vitiated Establishment, but would rejoice in returning to a pure one. To express it otherwise — we are the advocates for a national recognition and national support of religion — and we are not Voluntaries.'[4]

So, there was a fundamental difference between these Presbyterian churches in their view of church/state relations. The views were, indeed, irreconcilable. Notwithstanding this, there were those in the Free Church in the early 1860s who felt that moves might be made towards the United Presbyterian Church with a view to ascertaining the possibilities of the denominations moving closer together, or even eventually uniting with one another. A joint committee on Union of the United Presbyterians and the Free Church was appointed in

1863. From that point the Free Church at least was rent with controversy. Problems were raised not just over the different position of the United Presbyterians on the question of the civil magistrate, but also matters of doctrine and education.

There were many in the Free Church who saw the Establishment Principle as only a theoretical one for the church, as the denomination was practically only supported by voluntary contributions with no reliance upon state endowments. Others, however, saw that principle as one that was biblical and a fundamental part of the church's constitution. They were not prepared, therefore, to entertain any position that left the principle an 'open' question. Among these was George Smeaton. Many other prominent Disruption ministers and professors entertained scruples on that score. Opposition to the union was also actively supported by professors James Buchanan, John Duncan, James Gibson and James MacGregor, and by such prominent ministers as James Begg, Andrew and Horatius Bonar, Alexander Moody Stuart, Hugh Martin, Julius Wood and William Nixon.

George Smeaton had initially entertained the idea that a union between the churches was feasible, without the abandonment of Free Church principles. He was, it seems, influenced otherwise by conversations on the subject with Dr William Cunningham before the latter's death in 1861. In a letter to Mrs Cunningham dated 6 July 1869, Smeaton said: 'On the subject of union between the Free Church and the United Presbyterian Church, I felt much interest, and at that time I entertained the idea that it was feasible without an abandonment of Free Church principles to bring it about.' The last time the two divines conferred on the subject, Cunningham apparently said, 'I hope it will never be in my day.' To this Smeaton remarked that it must be possible to arrive at a union on a proper footing preserving Free Church principles. Cunningham, however, 'plainly intimated a different opinion, adding, "Not that I think there are sufficient reasons in that case for keeping the churches permanently separate.

But I shrink from the negotiations, my whole nature recoils from them.'"[5]

In previously accepting the feasibility of union with the United Presbyterians, Smeaton had not envisaged any disavowal of the Establishment Principle as any part of such an arrangement. The question was: How could a union be achieved without the sacrifice of Free Church principle? When it became evident that there were many in the Free Church who thought the denial of the Establishment Principle by the United Presbyterians was no bar to union, it was clear that Smeaton would oppose the union. The turning point in the debate was the General Assembly of 1867 when things became polarized and it became clear that the majority in the Free Church was prepared to make the Establishment Principle an open question.

Following the 1867 Assembly decision that there was 'no bar' to union in principle, Smeaton took a more distinct and prominent position on the anti-union side. In an Edinburgh Free Presbytery debate on Wednesday, 26 February 1868, he moved an overture which expressed his position clearly: 'Whereas it appears that the negotiating churches are not sufficiently ripe or prepared for enjoying the advantages of a cordial workable union; and whereas the further prosecution of these negotiations will only issue in disunion — it is humbly overtured by the Free Presbytery of Edinburgh to the General Assembly to suspend the negotiations for union in the present circumstances, and to substitute co-operation for incorporating union.'[6]

Smeaton said in the debate that he belonged, at that point, to neither party on the subject — pro- nor anti-union. Nevertheless he proposed the suspension of 'these fruitless negotiations, and that the churches should at present content themselves with a federative union, as the only thing that could be done at once, without creating a difficulty on either side'. One of his concerns at this stage was the threat of the oppression of a minority by a majority on the issue, just to force through a union about which a minority entertained scruples on principle.

Between 1868 and 1870 the movement for union in the Free Church was approached cautiously, but in 1870 the matter was stirred by a resolution of the General Assembly that the reports be sent down to presbyteries, instructing them to give special attention to their opinion as to whether there was any objection in principle to the formation of an incorporating union among the negotiating churches on the basis of the doctrinal standards of the churches in question.

There were, of course, other objections to the union apart from the matter of the Establishment Principle. As early as 1865, serious questions had been raised over whether or not the United Presbyterians held unambiguously to definite, or limited, atonement. It was believed by some in the Free Church that there had been a weakening of Calvinism in the United Presbyterian Church in the wake of a controversy within the Secession churches between 1841 and 1845.

James MacGregor, professor of systematic theology in New College, raised this doctrinal issue again in 1870 in a telling pamphlet entitled, 'The question of principle now raised in the Free Church specially regarding the atonement'.[7] MacGregor suggested that there was a toleration of Amyraldism in the United Presbyterian Church — a toleration, in his view, not allowed in the Free Church standards.[8]

In a recent study on the subject, Ian Hamilton has shown that there was considerable strength to MacGregor's argument, indicating as it did an erosion of Calvinist orthodoxy among the Secession churches in Scotland of the nineteenth century.[9] To MacGregor and others, this doctrinal matter had been played down in the Free Church.[10] George Smeaton did not directly focus on this aspect of the union controversy until the later debate in the Assembly of 1873. He was, however, aware of the issue. At a meeting of the Edinburgh Free Presbytery to deal with the union matter, on Tuesday, 8 November 1870, he seconded a motion of Professor Mac-

Gregor, who highlighted that matter in his speech in resisting the further moves towards incorporating union.[11] In the event, a majority in the presbytery voted for the motion, 'that there is no objection in principle to the proposed union', and the controversy rumbled on.[12]

George Smeaton made some effective contributions against the union and in defence of ecclesiastical establishments and national religion. On 25 October 1870, in what was described as a 'Great Anti-Union Meeting in Glasgow' under the auspices of a 'Free Church Defence Association', he gave a stirring speech on the subject of the movement towards union. In the speech he gives four objections to the proposed union:

> (1) 'I object to the whole proposal, as involving a great sin, because rendering necessary a betrayal of a great truth.' It was Smeaton's conviction that it would involve the Free Church effectively falling from a clear confession of the headship of Christ over nations.
>
> (2) 'I have an objection on constitutional grounds.' He did not consider it competent for any of the church courts to change the doctrines of the church, without the consent of the *whole* Free Church community.
>
> (3) 'Another objection, not less fatal, is: politics have as much to do with it — I fear much more to do with it — than religion.' He felt that the union movement had progressed 'in an atmosphere of strong political partisanship', and seemed 'destined to be a tool, and a willing tool, for the purpose of mere party politicians'. 'I tremble at the thought; for never does a church make the religion of Jesus a mere means to an ulterior end of a worldly kind but it brings down a terrible nemesis and visitation.'
>
> (4) 'There is a proposal to remove the key-stone from the Free Church which binds all together.' Smeaton felt that, as a church, the Free Church had 'professed the

ultimate truth on the whole subject of the relations between church and State' and so a decline from such a
position involved removing something crucial in the
confession of a church.[13]

Smeaton produced a significant pamphlet in 1871. His
National Christianity and Scriptural Union opens up the
whole matter of church/state relations in the light of the Bible
and church history. Central is the headship of Christ over
nations. He maintains that, 'Christ's headship over nations
includes his legislative and moral dominion over them, and is
a great biblical doctrine, irrespective of any symbolical recognition that has ever been given to it.'[14]

In relation to the Establishment idea, he says that without
maintaining this principle the church would, '…no longer be
in the position of being able to affirm ecclesiastically, whatever may be the private views of individuals, that nations can
recognize or distinguish truth from error; no longer in the
position of affirming that the central truths of Christianity,
incorporated in a church, may be established; no longer
capable of asking national funds to aid in the diffusion of the
gospel, and maintain it where it is. This is to revolutionize the
Free Church constitution. This is to put ourselves in a false
position to the historic Church of Scotland, and to repudiate
our own distinctly uttered testimony as well as the testimony
of our fathers.'[15]

This may seem to be a rather esoteric or even irrelevant
principle, not least in the light of our increasingly secular state.
The principle seems entirely ideological. But provided there
are adequate safeguards for the spiritual independence of the
church, against the interference of the State in church affairs,
the principle may be seen to be of the utmost practical
importance for a church to maintain. Smeaton put it this way:
Those maintaining this principle held, '…that there must be a
close connection between religion and all organized civil
society; that this was essential, if not to the being, at least to

its well-being; and that the diffusion of Christianity ought to be an object of the deepest interest to every ruler having at heart the peace, the prosperity, and the welfare of the nation over which he is placed.'[16]

Thinkers like Smeaton happily maintained that nations were under obligation to recognize the true religion and aid its diffusion by wise and salutary laws, and that rulers are bound to give civil sanction to the truth; to establish the church; and to contribute from the national resources, for the furtherance of the gospel. From a later address on 'The Scottish theory of ecclesiastical establishments', Smeaton summarized the position in this way:

> The State, considered in its corporate character, is a moral person, with a moral standing and responsibility. It is not the creation of the so-called social compact or of the popular will, but a divine institution based on natural religion. It coheres by a moral and religious bond; and its rulers are the lieutenants of God. If the State is a moral person, capable of performing duty, of committing sin, and suffering punishment, which every one must own who traces the fate of nations according to the divine word, it follows that a nation, acting by its rulers, can accept Christianity and make a public profession of it as the national rule and guide. It had been held together previous to the recognition of Christianity by some form of religion however impure, without which it could not have existed. And the first duty of the civil ruler when brought in contact with Christianity and persuaded of its divine origin is to receive the Bible as a revelation in a national way. The immediate effect of this is that it constitutes the State a Christian state, and pledges it to purge out its previous religion in the same way as pagan and Mohammedan nations constituted themselves, according to their false religions, or as the

atheistic state was constituted, or rather attempted to be constituted, by the French Convention.

A nation must have a religion, and the only question is, which it will adopt. And when Christianity comes to the nation, or to the family, it does not frown on either of these institutions, which also are divine in origin, but enters into them with an elevating purifying power, and sweetly coalesces with all that is purely human in both. These ordinances of God now became vessels by which Christianity is diffused. The national recognition of the Bible as a revelation subjecting the nation to its authority, though a great step gained, does not exhaust the nation's duty, as widely diverging views prevail upon the right interpretation of the Bible. The State must by the necessity of the case adopt a creed which will commonly be prepared by the church. The same duty that devolves upon an individual Christian confronts a Christian state, and it naturally appends the civil sanction to the church's creed. It must distinguish between scripture truth and its perversion. The State, by the adoption of a creed, gives utterance to the self-consciousness of a Christian community. It confesses the Christianity it has adopted... The nation, acting by its rulers, must needs adopt a creed, and so distinguish between truth and error in the confession which it makes. It must be Trinitarian or Unitarian, Protestant or Popish, Calvinistic or Arminian, by the necessity of the position. These diverging lines of profession cannot be ignored. More than that; the responsible rulers must proclaim a Christian constitution and adopt a legislation all through the nation's history upon the principles of revelation. A Christian state is competent to make the same confession of its faith that an individual makes.[17]

Smeaton was, therefore, strongly on the anti-union side in the controversy that engulfed and nearly split the church in the years 1863-73 and on the anti-disestablishment side when that matter arose in the non-established churches after 1874.

A threat of a split in the church in 1872 persuaded the leaders of the majority pro-union party to drop the proposals for incorporating union in the interests of maintaining a unity, such as it might be, within the Free Church ranks. As Charles M'Crie put it in his authoritative book, *The Church of Scotland: Her Divisions and her Reunions*: 'Continuance of negotiations became of more doubtful expediency when opposition to union with the United Presbyterian Church was approved of and actively taken part in by professors John Duncan, George Smeaton, James Macgregor and James Gibson; by such ministers as Dr Andrew Bonar, Dr Forbes, Dr Miller and Mr Ralph Smith of Glasgow, by Dr Horatius Bonar, Dr Moody Stuart and Dr Hugh Martin of Edinburgh; all these acting in concert with Dr Julius Wood at Dumfries, Mr John James Bonar at Greenock, Mr Nixon at Montrose and Mr Patrick Borrowman at Glencairn. Surely it was better, far better, to suspend negotiations with a sister church than to force such men to separate from the church they loved and had served so long.'[18]

However, proposals for a mutual eligibility scheme by which United Presbyterian ministers might be called to Free Church congregations (and vice versa) were brought forward into the 1873 General Assembly. This was seen by the anti-unionists as union by the back door, and it was strenuously opposed in the 1873 Assembly in view of the fact that the 'mutual eligibility' was not specifically on the basis of accepting the Free Church Formula of 1846, including its preamble.

In the run up to the critical 1873 General Assembly, George Smeaton wrote to *The Watchword* magazine with an impassioned plea for prayer in the crisis faced by the church. He wrote in these terms: 'Let us pray that the church may be jealous, as in her days of first love, for the honour of her Lord, and only afraid of what may dishonour him. Pray that the church may take no step which shall directly or indirectly prove a denial of her Lord, that she may not fall away from attained truth, that she may not be unfaithful to her past testimony to Christ's special atonement and headship over nations, and that the great Scottish principle as to the mutual harmony of church and State, and their independence in their several spheres, vindicated only in our land, and fitted, to be a light to all lands, may not be compromised or betrayed. Pray that honoured brethren may not be left to follow any false rule of duty, such as self-made interpretations of providence which run counter to a plain text of Scripture, and that none may permit themselves to be ensnared by casuistical questions, when the true point at issue is the maintenance of divine truth, and the ecclesiastical confession of it.'[19]

Smeaton was a member of that 1873 Assembly and, in seconding a motion of William Nixon (Montrose) against the proposals, he made one of his rare speeches in the General Assembly. The concern of Nixon's motion was that the terms of the 1846 Act, including its preamble, must form part of any arrangement to admit probationers or ministers from other denominations to any Free Church congregation. In this way assent would be required to the basic constitutional principles of the church. In his supporting speech, George Smeaton pointed to the two issues in which there were serious differences between the United Presbyterian Church and the Free Church, namely, the duty of nations and their rulers to the church of Christ, and the matter of the extent of the atonement. It was clear to Smeaton that:

> ...The two larger churches, judging by their public documents, are separated by a wide, yawning and impassable gulf. As to the first of these great doctrines — Christ's authority over nations and national duty to him — will any man affirm that the churches are at one, if he has read the U.P. statement on disestablishment, and observed on what terms it was received by the whole synod? I thought such a phenomenon as the

U.P. manifesto would have staggered our friends in the
majority. But no: all these men are to be eligible. I
ask — what is to become of all that body of truth which
we have so long taught upon divine authority as to the
duty of nations and their rulers?

As to the other great doctrine — the doctrine of the
atonement — what satisfaction have we obtained?
None. I am ready to prove at any one moment that the
United Presbyterian Church ... not merely allows, but
adopts the doctrine of universal atonement, irrespective
of any distinction between elect and non-elect ... an
error fatal to all Calvinistic churches, because operating
backwards and forwards in the most subverting way —
backwards upon election, and forwards on all sound
views of conversion. I never will consent to legalize this
error in the church...[20]

Smeaton movingly went on to say that if the overture as it
stood — allowing mutual eligibility without specifically requir-
ing acceptance of Free Church principles — were to be
accepted, he would no longer regard the church as the church
into which he was ordained and had vowed obedience in the
Lord because it would be accepting voluntarism as an integral
part of its constitution. He even spoke at one point of finding
himself outside the pale of the church over this issue and
ended his speech with a moving appeal: 'This church seems
determined to make room for voluntarism, and to gain this
you are, in effect, whether you intend it or not, casting us out.
Those who stood shoulder to shoulder with you at the Disruption are now to be ejected in effect, whether this be intended
or not, that this theory may have full scope and free course
among you. Be it so. I believe the Free Church is committing
a great sin; but I believe also that the wonderful Counsellor,
who is above all the schemes and plans of men, will dispose it
for his glory and for the vindication of his truth. And to him,

the Lord of the church, I appeal with all humility. Arise, O
Lord, and plead thine own cause.'[21]

The matter was unresolved at the end of the sederunt
which lasted seven hours that day (Wednesday, 28 May).[22] It
was clear that there was the possibility of a breach in Free
Church ranks over the issue. As a result of a conference in
between times among some of the leaders of the pro-union
party, Robert S. Candlish, in one of his last acts in a General
Assembly,[23] came back in the evening with a modified motion
in which to a large extent the concerns of the anti-unionists
were met. That modification saved the day as far as a split
was concerned, but Nixon, Smeaton and many other ministers and elders recorded their dissent on the basis that (1) the
deliverance contained an unqualified approval of the reports
of the committee on union; (2) the declaration relative to the
headship of Christ over nations was inadequate; and (3)
because the mutual eligibility overture was made the permanent law of the church. In all, 132 ministers and elders dissented from the decision of the Assembly on the matter of
mutual eligibility, out of a total of around 600 commissioners.
This, however, was effectively the end of the union negotiations for the time being, and there was a sense of relief among
the anti-unionist minority that the constitutional position of
the church largely remained intact.

Throughout the controversy, although the position es-
poused by Smeaton and other constitutionalists grew in the
support received, it was always a minority, being never more
than a third of the whole Assembly. When moves were made
some twenty years later for union between the Free Church
and the United Presbyterian Church, the number of 'constitutionalists' in the Free Church was greatly reduced. The union
of these churches took place in 1900, though essentially it was
a result of a theological weakening reflected in Declaratory
Acts in the United Presbyterian Church (1879) and the Free
Church (1892). A tiny minority in the Free Church remained
out of that union and fought their case through the law courts

to be considered the true Free Church, and rightful possessors of the properties and endowments of the old church. Central in their arguments was the fact that the Free Church, in order to bring about the union, had sacrificed the Establishment Principle. In effect this won the day, finally, in the House of Lords in 1904. The minority adopted the position advocated by George Smeaton and others. Smeaton, too, had taken issue with the Declaratory Act of the United Presbyterian Church (1879), about which he remarked to a friend, 'There are good Calvinists in the United Presbyterian synod; but I should not find it difficult to prove that in its Declaratory Statement the synod has taken up Arminian ground.'[24]

In 1875 George Smeaton gave a spirited defence of the Establishment Principle at a meeting of the Glasgow Conservative Association in Glasgow. The address was later published under the title, *The Scottish Theory of Ecclesiastical Establishments*, which in many respects is a mini-classic of Scottish theology. This pamphlet of thirty-five pages was strongly promoted by the Conservative Association, which invited all recipients of the pamphlet to take further copies for distribution. Quantities of not less than 100 would be available from the Association's rooms at a cost of one pound — including postage![25] The context of the address was the agitation within the non-established churches in Scotland for disestablishment of the Church of Scotland. Smeaton was opposed to this movement, and voted accordingly in debates on the issue in the 1879 and 1882 General Assemblies, in rare visits to the Assembly. His position on this was well summarized in an obituary notice: '[He] had ... no sympathy with the disestablishment agitation, not because of any particular love of the Establishment itself, but because the movement was likely to lead to the removal from the statute-books of the State recognition of religion which had been embedded in the Constitution since the Reformation.'[26]

In this connection it is interesting to report that in 2005 — 130 years after Smeaton's address on religious establishments to the Conservative Association in Glasgow — the United Kingdom government put forward a bill entitled 'Incitement to religious hatred'. Such a bill, if enacted, far from advancing the Christian religion, in effect would have made an outspoken promotion of the exclusive claims of Christian faith as against other faiths, all the more difficult.[27] In the event, the 'Religious hatred bill' was modified by a House of Lords amendment in the House of Commons on 31 January 2006. This narrowed the scope of the law and introduced a broad protection for free speech. However, in a secular society which fails to acknowledge the primacy of Christian faith, all sorts of legislation will appear which may be quite antagonistic to Christian principles, not least in education and morals.

In hindsight, as one seeks to assess the issues in which Smeaton and others on the anti-union side became so passionately involved, one might wonder what all the fuss was about. Why was Smeaton so adamant about the Establishment Principle and the national recognition of Christianity? Since his day our society has become 'multicultural' and secular. But of course that in a sense is the point. Smeaton abhorred the development, implicit for example in the French Revolution, of the 'secular state'. He felt the church must speak with a crystal clear voice against any tendency of the state to be established on secular lines. The church, at least, will look for the establishment of true Christianity in a nation and will work and pray to that end.

Smeaton saw that this had far-reaching significance not only for the church, but also for the family and for education. There is a passage in his speech at the Anti-Union Meeting in Glasgow that is clear-sighted and prophetic, and which puts the importance of what he maintained in clear perspective:

> Christianity does not contemplate men as so many units or individuals having no organic connection. The great matter, indeed, is the personal salvation of the individual; but Christianity does not end there. It entered the

world finding two divine institutions already existing —
the family and the State — and originating a third, the
Christian church; and all three are put under the law to
Christ. Of course, no true Christian has any difficulty as
to Christ's headship over the church, nor any difficulty
as to the family, which it is allowed on all hands must
be put under the law to Christ, as soon as they who rule
the family become Christian... The State becomes a
Christian state just as the family becomes a Christian
family, and it would be strange indeed if all divine institutions were not capable of taking in the new divine
element, and of being ennobled and exalted by it.[28]

A State, then, can, and in a real sense should, become a
'Christian state', with a distinctively Christian creed. As to the
nature of the creed, Smeaton says in one place that it might
even be akin to the basis of the Evangelical Alliance, as then
constituted, in order, that is, to avoid sectarianism. 'The creed
of the nation may be said to be comprehended in that of the
four Councils [i.e. Nicea (AD 325), Constantinople (AD 381),
Ephesus (AD 431), and Chalcedon (AD 451)], and in the
Protestant faith common to Protestant countries; and future
statesmen will probably establish these; that is establish
something like the Articles of the Evangelical Alliance,
whether in one corporate connection or another, rather than
take in all the peculiarities of one selected or favoured
church.'[29]

The State and the church, he maintained, on biblical
grounds, should always recognize the headship of Christ.
Smeaton of course was aware that, 'Many things are always
occurring to throw it [the State] back to its heathen condition.'
Interestingly, and significantly in relation to events in the
United Kingdom since his day, Smeaton very clearly brings
out something of the significance of such a throwing back to a
heathen, or we may say, purely secular condition: 'Thus you
may advocate the absolute separation of the school from the

church, and of religious education from secular education, till it comes to this — and it has come to this both in England and Scotland — that the Bible, God's own voice from heaven, is simply excluded from the school. That is to heathenize the State. You may carry out the separation of church and State to such lengths as to assert that the State is to have no alliance with the church. That is to heathenize the State — maintaining, as it does, that the State is an institution incapable of alliance with the Christian church…'[30]

The combined effects of the disestablishment agitation in the late nineteenth century and the Education (Scotland) Act of 1872, by which the Protestant church schools were passed over to the state system, gave impetus to the 'secular state' which has increasingly dominated political and educational philosophy in this country ever since. Kenneth Ross, in his fine study of the Free Church Case of 1900-04, makes a very perceptive comment about the significance of the shift in attitudes on the Establishment Principle in the Free Church:

For all her endeavour in home mission, the development of the Free Church was characterized by a subtle abdication of national responsibility and a growing complacency in her role as a great denomination. She grew complacent too in her assumption that there was no real threat to the influence of the church in Scottish society. When the April number of the Church of Scotland *Missionary Record* suggested in 1872 that the removal of the privileges of the Established church might result in, among other things, a secular system of education where the authority of Scripture would not be accepted, profanity being permitted in the press, Bible laws about marriage and divorce being abrogated, and in the observance of Sunday being wholly abolished, the *Presbyterian* for the following month dismissed the suggestion as 'this bosh'. They [i.e. the Free Church] did not see the yawning gulf of the 'modern schism'. In welcoming the new *denominational* role of the church, they complied with the process of secularization. It might be said that they were unconscious accomplices in the marginalization of the church.[31]

Besides this, the apparent lack of concern for the doctrinal issues in the Free Church, especially in relation to the extent of the atonement, is also of significance. In the Free Church this came to fruition in a Declaratory Act of 1892. This Act indicated the weakening of historic Calvinism which had been evident 'under the surface' in the Union Controversy of 1863-73. Very often a weakening or compromise of truths once firmly held accompanies such movements for 'organic union'. The issues are more far-reaching than they may at first seem to be.

These points were not lost on George Smeaton. He was a man of charitable disposition. He was not averse to friendly, co-operative and even federal relations with other churches, where that was possible. But he did not wish to see the dissipation of the established principles and practices of the Reformed church. At any rate these principles and practices were his life-long commitment.

It has to be said, of course, that the influence of the church in the land did not just depend on an Establishment arrangement, but also on the spiritual strength of the church itself. Unfortunately there was a movement in the churches, not least through the Free Church, in the late Victorian society, which tended to undermine the power and integrity of the church's witness in terms of biblical authority and orthodoxy. The matter of biblical criticism was another issue of the day which exercised George Smeaton.

9.
Bible criticism

The integrity of biblical
religion rests on a source
which is utterly reliable
and historically accurate.
It is one of Smeaton's
legacies to the church
that he saw this
connection in his day...

9.
Bible criticism

The Free Church was beset by one controversy after another throughout the 1870s. All the major issues were of deep concern to George Smeaton. We have considered his involvement in the Union controversy on the anti-union side. On the back of that controversy was one of perhaps even more far-reaching significance for the health and strength of the church as a spiritual force. It had to do with the shift in attitude to the Bible itself as an inspired and trustworthy record. From the earlier part of the century, especially on the Continent, theories had been propounded of Bible criticism, as applied to the Old Testament, which questioned the historicity and trustworthiness of the books that comprised the accepted canon of Old Testament Scripture.

Such views crept into the Free Church almost unawares through the teaching of Andrew Bruce Davidson (1831-1902). Davidson had been licensed in 1856 but had never received a call to any congregation. He apparently engaged in critical studies, imbibing the views on the Old Testament then becoming current in Germany and elsewhere. This appealed to him, and to others, as 'progressive' and scholarly.

In John 'Rabbi' Duncan's declining years it was felt by the church that he could use an assistant in the Old Testament department in the New College. So Davidson was appointed as lecturer/assistant to Duncan in 1863. He was elected professor after the death of the 'Rabbi' in 1870.[1] It was he, says Principal John Macleod, who became 'an alien infusion in Old Testament studies in Scotland'. Macleod adds, tellingly, 'Robertson Smith caught the infection and spread the plague.'[2]

If Davidson was somewhat diffident and cautious in his approach, William Robertson Smith (1846-94), his prize student in the years 1866-70, was far more bold, outspoken and even arrogant in pushing the critical views. It was said and believed that Smith was a brilliant student and scholar. However, his systematic theology professor in New College, the orthodox but eccentric James MacGregor (1830-94) — a native Gaelic speaker, incidentally — was arguably closer to the mark when he later described Smith in this way: 'The Cambridge Arabic professor is found to be in his thinking receptive rather than originative, taking his philosophy from Herbert Spencer, his social archaeology from J. F. Maclennan, and his biblical criticism from the Continental school represented by Wellhausen.' MacGregor adds, '...In a mind so constituted and furnished there are found the same traits of unfitness for veritable criticism [i.e. judgement] as elsewhere are found in that master — rash arbitrariness in assumptions even as to fact, ignorance or ignoring of information outside the "cave" of a one-sided book-learning, and manifested incapacity for simply independent judgement on the ground of relevant evidence.'[3] In other words, in MacGregor's view Smith had seriously flawed presuppositions in his approach to the critical issues!

Lightning struck the Free Church at the end of 1875 with the publication of a volume of the *Encyclopaedia Britannica* (ninth edition), containing an article from Robertson Smith entitled 'Bible' in which radical higher critical views were evident. From this point the issue of biblical criticism and the nature of divine inspiration convulsed the Free Church until in 1881 Smith was removed from his Chair in the Aberdeen College. He had been appointed to the Old Testament Chair there immediately after the completion of his studies at New College in 1870. He was barely twenty-five years of age!

Included in the same volume of the *Encyclopaedia Britannica* was an article on 'Angels', also by Robertson Smith, which was also found objectionable by many in the church. Broadly speaking, this article raised the question of whether

or not Robertson Smith even believed in the existence of
angels at all. There was no reference either to the Devil or to
fallen angels. Given the clear teaching in Scripture on such
matters, this position of Smith's was rightly seen to be an
alarming one to many within the church. Smeaton brought
the issue into focus in his dissent from the committee's report
in 1877: 'The angel of Jehovah is not allowed to have a
personal subsistence, and in the description of angels generally, nothing is said in the way of affirming their personality,
their intellectual and moral qualities, and their agency as
ministering spirits. On the other hand, they are represented as
a portion of poetic and prophetic imagery.'[4] Apart from this,
Smeaton also took issue with the fact that Smith made no
allusion to the character and activity of the fallen angels. By
any measure these were extremely serious deficiencies. It
indicated a tendency to minimize if not altogether to exclude
the supernatural element in Christian faith.

As to Smith's views expressed in the article 'Bible', A. C.
Cheyne summarizes the issues succinctly:

> Smith's published article assumed that the Scripture
> narratives which we now possess are not the originals
> but later, edited versions of accounts dating from vari-
> ous periods in Jewish history. In particular, it contended
> that the 'Mosaic' legislation had first been promulgated,
> if not actually composed, during Israel's exile in Baby-
> lon (hundreds of years after Moses) and under the in-
> fluence of the great eighth-century prophets: its attribu-
> tion to Moses was not fraudulent, of course, but simply
> in accord with the recognized literary conventions of the
> age. The article also suggested that most of the psalms
> had not been written by David, eliminated much of the
> predictive element in the prophets, and denied author-
> ship of the Gospels to the evangelists whose names
> they bear. In sum, it required no extraordinary insight
> to realize that Smith's picture of the Bible, and of the

Old Testament in particular, deviated very considerably from that which had long held sway in Scotland.[5]

Smith's views were generally in line with the Graf-Keunen-Wellhausen scheme. Smith made no reference to the supernatural origin of the Bible. He accepted the 'documentary hypothesis' as far as the first four books of the Bible were concerned, treating them as being pieced together from various sources and not at all the work of Moses. As to the book of Deuteronomy, this he considered to be a post-exilic prophetic 'personation' of Moses. He played down the prophetic element in the prophets. In relation to the New Testament, Smith denied that the synoptic Gospels were written by those whose names they bear; they were, rather, 'non-apostolic digests of spoken and written apostolic tradition'.

These were issues of great concern to George Smeaton. In his *Scottish Theology*, John Macleod states in one place that when 'Rabbi' Duncan discerned that his junior colleague A. B. Davidson was going off on rationalistic directions in his Old Testament teaching, the older man apparently 'called in the help of Smeaton to do what he could to reclaim him'.[6] Though there is no documentary evidence for this, nevertheless it is quite clear that Smeaton took very serious issue with the views of Robertson Smith, and therefore also with Smith's master, his colleague in New College. When the matter of the higher criticism received currency publicly through Robertson Smith's articles in the *Encyclopaedia Britannica* from 1875, Smeaton did, however, take a strong stand.

First of all he wrote an impassioned plea to the younger man from New College. 'I would beseech you to pause, to take counsel with your father and your seniors', he said, 'before committing yourself to positions from which you will find it every day more difficult to recede. Who has not been drawn — if he has thought at all — into speculations and opinions on which he now looks back with contempt and grief? The peril is in a public committal to crude notions. I wish I could do something to rescue a gifted young mind and save it for the future usefulness which we all fondly anticipated.'[7] Smeaton appealed to a fatiguing experience of more than forty years' reading of the higher criticism, and expressed his surprise that Smith's mathematical mind should find any attraction in that barren field: 'Are not the theories without any basis of solid historical fact? And what is the worth of such theories where the basis is mere conjecture or petty internal criticism leaping to arbitrary conclusions? I hope your mind will soon revolt from this castle-building in the clouds... In the meantime,' Smeaton goes on, 'the matter is serious. I fear that many a Christian's mind has been shocked by your inconsiderate attack on what is regarded as sacred, and it will not mend the matter to reflect on "a weak faith" either on the part of the simple Christian mind, or of the practical ministerial mind. We, as professors, are not appointed by the church to teach what tends to shake the faith of any, or to advocate a criticism which is not legitimate.'[8]

Smith's article, according to his old teacher, was the first instance of an attack from within any Scottish church on the genuineness of the Bible. He had imitated the 'chartered audacity' of Germany and Holland, and, though perhaps he did not himself practise the worst excesses of the Tübingen school, there was the gravest danger in naturalizing such views in Scotland. 'I cannot suppose', Smeaton continued, 'that the sad and bitter harvest produced by that criticism in such men as Baur, Schwegler, Hilgenfeld, Schenkel, Keim, Scholten, Kuenen, and others still more extreme, can find much approval in your own mind. But where will it stop if it is legitimated? There will arise others much more extreme than you, as a Strauss arose out of the school of Baur, and how could we suppress it, if we make all criticism legitimate? Nay, how could we check it in the pulpit when the pupils go further than their teacher? Would you like to hear your own pupils saying from the pulpit that Matthew was 'non-apostolic' and consequently of no authority because not an eye-witness?'[9]

Smeaton's position, then, was clear enough. But he did not leave the matter just by way of private counsel. He tells the young professor: 'I may have to act against these opinions being made open questions in the church, but I implore you to save us all from this painful alternative.'[10]

Generally speaking, the older orthodox professors and ministers were simply ignored or marginalized by the supposedly 'progressive' scholars and their supporters. In a recent study of William Robertson Smith and the celebrated case in the Free Church, the author only refers to Smeaton's letter to Smith. He says that the interest of the letter does not lie in any arguments it contains, as there were none, but in the raw emotions evident — pain, repugnance, incredulity and panic. He is scornful of Smeaton, saying that he had 'no understanding of the meaning or purpose of the higher criticism, as conceived by Smith'.[11] No doubt anyone who dared to demur from the findings of the critical views just would not have any understanding of them! But it was simply not true. Smeaton recognized all too well the nature and the potential outcome of the views Smith advocated. It is as if the critics were the only really capable scholars.

Unfortunately, the rising generation of ministers in the Free Church were generally impatient with the confessional theology and conservative approach to the Scriptures, and seeds were sown which would undermine the fabric of the faith in the eyes of the world. This was something not clearly understood by Robertson Smith and other such critics, who may well have thought they were doing God's work. But that was one of the illusions of the epoch.

Smeaton at any rate was true to his warning to the young scholar. He was part of the college committee which met from 1876 onwards to deal with the matters raised by Smith's writings. He also was one of a sub-committee of seven appointed on 19 September 1876. The first draft report of this sub-committee was made public on 17 January 1877.

The sub-committee examined the article 'Bible' and also considered an article on 'Angels' which had also been found objectionable, at least by the conservative men. The opinion prevailed among the majority on the sub-committee, however, that there was no *prima facie* case for heresy against the professor, though it felt that his critical opinions were scarcely compatible with his position as a teacher of divinity students. Smeaton objected to this. He maintained that it was not enough simply to express regret or concern over the appearance of the negative criticism from Germany within the church. 'Nor is it enough,' he writes in his dissent to the final report which went up to the General Assembly later that year, 'Nor is it enough to accept a mere profession of loyalty to the principles of the church as a sufficient reason for abstaining from further action.'[12]

The report of the committee stated that it had 'not found in the article [i.e. on 'Bible'] any ground to support a process for heresy'. Smeaton did not agree, and dissented accordingly: 'One may not find, according to the technical use of the term heresy, any direct attack on a fundamental article of faith, while he finds error enough to call for judicial action and severe repression on the part of the church.'[13] He uses the example of Arminianism and quotes William Ames, who recognized that it was not properly a heresy, but was, nonetheless a 'dangerous error', and therefore should not claim a legitimate position in a Reformed church.

In relation to the negative criticism, Smeaton saw it in this way: It was said that the negative criticism [i.e. the so-called 'higher criticism'] could be separated from the underlying philosophy, but he was not convinced they could be sundered. While in one generation there may be acceptance of a certain inter-weaving of supernatural elements, how could one have confidence that future generations would not yield to the basic anti-supernatural philosophy behind the sort of criticism proposed? And then the question arose about the impact of all this on the doctrine of the inspiration of the

Scripture. 'Not only so,' says Smeaton, 'opinions which are fatal to inspiration, dislocating the unity of Scripture, and undermining the canonical rank of several books of Scripture on petty grounds of internal criticism, can only be called dangerous error tending to heresy.'[14]

In addition to this, Smeaton felt that Smith's 'explanation' of his views on prophecy was even more unsatisfactory than the original statement, showing, as he put it, an attitude of absolute indifference to the commentary of an inspired apostle. On the question of Smith's views of the synoptic Gospels, Smeaton also had strong objections. Smith had asserted, 'A considerable portion of the New Testament is made up of writings not directly apostolical, and a main problem of criticism is to determine the relation of these writings, especially the Gospels, to apostolic teaching and tradition.' Smeaton considered this 'very unguarded language'.[15] Summing up his position he was very clear: 'I hold that the doctrine of inspiration and Professor Smith's views are irreconcilable.'[16]

It is interesting to note that in his 'Refutation of Prof. W. Robertson Smith', written five years later, R. L. Dabney (1820-98) wrote to the same effect: 'No fair man doubts but that the *Confession of the Free Church*, Chap. I, §2, means to assert what Mr. Smith distinctly impugned touching the Old Testament canon.'[17] More recently, the Old Testament scholar Edward J. Young, of Westminster Theological Seminary, commented that Smith 'sought to accomplish the impossible task of reconciling the newer views of Wellhausen, which he himself essentially embraced, with the doctrine of inspiration stated in the first chapter of the Westminster Confession of Faith'.[18] The weaknesses in Robertson Smith's position, in the broadest terms, have been effectively exposed by Nigel Cameron: 'What is clear is that Robertson Smith succeeded in maintaining the "infallibility" of Scripture only by attenuating its sense to such a degree as to empty it of the distinctive meaning with which the theological tradition in which he stood has customarily associated it. The tensions and ambi-

guities which flow through his writings on the doctrine of
Scripture reveal a man who sought to hold together what
were inherently divergent ways of understanding revelation,
and faith, and the Bible.'[19]

Smeaton objects further to Smith's views on the book of
Deuteronomy and the Song of Solomon. Smith accepted the
'fraudulent personation theory' on the source of the book of
Deuteronomy, holding that it was not Mosaic, but rather a
composition dating from many years after Moses' death.
'Professor Smith must make his choice between the reception
of the book as an inspired revelation, with all that it purports to
be, as written at the time of Moses, and as the work of Moses,
or reject it altogether as a fraud, and entitled to no respect.'[20]
Smeaton reckoned that such a view of the book as Smith's was
tantamount to dropping it from the inspired canon. Smith
denied the 'spiritual sense' in the understanding of the Song of
Solomon. The book, to Smeaton, justified its rank as an
inspired and canonical book in relation to allusions in it to the
communion between the Bridegroom and the bride, that is to
say, Christ and the church. Treating it as merely an 'earthly
love-poem' will not do, to Smeaton at least.

Smeaton ends his dissent from the college committee's
report with a devastating criticism on the conclusions of the
report: 'An attack on the genuineness and authority of the
Scripture, whether dignified by the title of the higher criticism
or prompted by the lower scepticism, ought never to be
permitted within the church on the part of any office-bearer.
We can keep criticism within its proper limits, and this occasion may have been permitted to occur that we may show to
other churches how we can act in the exercise of our independent jurisdiction.'[21] The sad thing is that he was not
supported by anyone else on the committee, except, on the
matter of the article on 'Angels', by David Brown, professor of
New Testament exegesis in the Aberdeen College.[22]

In 1879, two years later, in a rare visit to the General Assembly, George Smeaton voted in support of a motion made

by Andrew Bonar in which the Aberdeen Presbytery were to be instructed to take immediate steps towards a libel against Robertson Smith, particularly with reference to his position of the book of Deuteronomy.[23] If sustained this would lead to the suspension of Smith from his functions, 'professional and ministerial and judicial'. The full motion read: 'The General Assembly instruct the Presbytery of Aberdeen to meet, and take immediate steps for having the libel, as regards the second particular of the first alternative charge, served in due form upon Professor Smith; they also instruct the Presbytery, in the event of their finding the libel sustained, either by the admission of Professor Smith, or by adequate proof, to suspend him from his functions, professorial and ministerial and judicial, till the next meeting of Assembly, reserving final judgement in the case till that meeting of Assembly; and the Assembly now appoint a committee to adjust the libel in this view, excluding from it all parts that are not now applicable, and report to a future diet of this Assembly.'

The 'second particular of the first alternative charge' was the accusation that Professor Smith promulgated 'the opinion that the book of inspired Scripture called Deuteronomy, which is confessedly an historical record, does not possess that character, but was made to assume it by a writer of a much later age, who therein, in the name of God, presented, in dramatic form, instructions and laws as proceeding from the mouth of Moses, though these never were, and never could have been, uttered by him'.[24] The motion carried by one vote (321-320),[25] though the matter was overtaken by events and a process of fudging the issue.

Smith survived the Assembly debate on his case the following May, but shortly after that 1880 Assembly there appeared another offensive article from his pen in the *Encyclopaedia Britannica* entitled 'Hebrew language and literature'. This exacerbated the situation. Robertson Smith was eventually removed from the Chair in the Aberdeen College, though not as a Free Church minister, by decision of the

1881 Assembly. This decision, however, was based not on any conviction about the error of the views stated, but on weak grounds of expediency. No charges were specified, and no guilt of heresy established. It was simply held that he lost the confidence of the church. Little wonder the supporters of Smith took it as a triumph for the critical positions. Smeaton, certainly, was grieved over this matter, as his later discussions on inspiration in his volume on the Holy Spirit indicate.

With special reference to the matter of the post-mosaic origin of the book of Deuteronomy, Smeaton later commented that, 'Those writers who attach themselves to the school of modern thought have recently declared that we find in Scripture instances of one man personating another — that the book of Deuteronomy, for example, is the fictitious personation of Moses by another man, and that too in the solemn position of professing to receive a divine revelation; and that the book was not composed till many centuries after Moses' death. The fraudulent personation theory is the lowest depth of criticism.'[26] 'Such theories', he goes on to say, 'are wholly inconsistent with the supposition of a man acting under the guidance of the Holy Spirit of God; and if they could be endured for a moment, would render inspiration impossible.'[27] A recent successor to Smeaton in the New Testament Chair in New College has commented that, 'Smeaton thought that the only alternatives were personation or authorship; he plumped for authorship. His students, convinced that Moses did not write Deuteronomy, opted for the mediating theology. Mediating theology became the guiding principle of his pupil Marcus Dods.'[28]

After his removal from the Chair in Aberdeen, and by all accounts at the request of — he claimed — six hundred prominent Free Churchmen, Robertson Smith gave a series of lectures entitled 'The Old Testament and the Jewish church'. It was a 'defence' of his position. In his 'Refutation of Prof. W. Robertson Smith,' R. L. Dabney characterizes Smith's position in this way: 'The object of the lectures is to disparage as much as possible the genuineness and authority of extensive parts of our Old Testament. To do this, the loose and rash methods of the most sceptical school of criticism are freely employed. But a worse trait is that the sounder criticism is usually disregarded and treated as non-existent.'[29]

Dabney goes on to write in a manner akin to Smeaton: 'This book may be justly described as thoroughly untrustworthy... Citations are warped, history misrepresented, other theologians' views adroitly travestied, half truths advanced for whole ones. All is dogmatic assertion. In the construing of Scripture statements, the author, as if he were the critical pope, discards expositions which do not suit his purpose, however well supported by critical learning and the greatest names, without giving reasons for his decrees... Everything which does not please him is absolutely uncritical.'[30]

Subsequently Smith accepted the post of Lord Almoner's Readership in Arabic at Cambridge, becoming in turn a Fellow of Christ's College, university librarian, and ultimately Professor of Arabic. He never married, and for the rest of his short life he was more or less a closeted scholar. He died of tuberculosis in 1894.

Robertson Smith was undeniably highly influential in the development of liberal views of the Bible. His impact, however, was wider than in theology or biblical criticism. In his 1965 monograph on Sigmund Freud, the American scholar Rousas J. Rushdoony, for example, showed that the anthropology Freud went to, '...was ostensibly religious but actually naturalistic, namely, William Robertson Smith's (1846-94), whose works, in particular *The Religion of the Semites*, are basic to an understanding both of the nature and meaning of modernism in the churches and of Freudianism as a psychology.'[31]

Norman Madsen points out how Smeaton, by contrast to the critical developments in the nineteenth century, held to what he describes as 'a literalistic interpretation of the Genesis creation stories'.[32] 'For Smeaton,' he observes, 'Adam was a real man who lived in space and time, and what the Bible states concerning Adam is undoubtedly true.'[33] As he has commented: 'Smeaton then not only maintains an orthodox Christology and doctrine of the Trinity, but he similarly retains essentially an orthodox anthropology.'[34] Consequently, with reference to the critical views prevalent in his day, 'He chose to reject this new scholarship and respect only the theology of antiquity.'[35] As Thomas Smith was to put it, while George Smeaton was 'personally intimate with many of the German critics, he was conversant with the writings of all. While he was ever ready to acknowledge the great amount of good that he found in their writings, he was happily able to discriminate between the corn and the chaff.'[36]

George Smeaton, then, was well aware of the trends in the church in biblical criticism. He was clearly aware of the growing acceptance of them. His own position on such issues was quite clear.[37] Like his friends James Begg, Andrew and Horatius Bonar and Alexander Moody Stuart, he had lived through the Disruption days only to find that forty years on the old orthodoxy was now largely despised. The church did not stand where it once stood. There had been a revolution, and it was a revolution, for all the 'promise' expected, which would sound the death-knell to much of church life in Scotland in the twentieth century in the wake of a liberal denial of Scripture authority and trustworthiness. The moving words of Smeaton's good friend, Alexander Moody Stuart, effectively summarize the impact of the critical movement for Scottish religious life: 'The word of the Lord is pure, and out of this trial will come forth in all its brightness as silver out of the furnace. But, meanwhile, an unutterable calamity may overtake us, for our children may lose the one treasure we are bound to bequeath to them; and for long years they may wander "through dry places seeking rest, and finding none", before they recover their hold of the Word of life, and regain their footing on the rock of eternal truth.'[38] Sadly, the regaining of such a footing is still awaited, in Scotland and beyond.

The downgrade had penetrated Scottish Presbyterianism largely through the Free Church, accompanied with claims that there was no denial of evangelical truth. In effect, biblical authority and infallibility were denied, and the framework of biblical faith was undermined. The issues involved are well highlighted by Kenneth Ross in his *Church and Creed in Scotland*: 'Given the force of the spreading naturalism of the late nineteenth-century thought, the instinct of faith scarcely seems an adequate defence for the integrity of a supernatural religion. Yet it was the very strength and conviction of their evangelical faith which persuaded [Marcus] Dods and others that their Christianity was impregnable. It blinded them to the fact that the concessions they made broke down the orthodox line of defence so that the essence of faith was exposed to serious danger. They never appreciated the magnitude of what was done in the 1889-92 period.'[39]

The strength of evangelical convictions of such men such as Marcus Dods and A. B. Bruce may be seriously questioned. Of these movements and men in the Free Church, the great English preacher, C. H. Spurgeon, an erstwhile admirer of the church, was to write these perceptive words in the year Dods succeeded George Smeaton at New College: 'The Free Church of Scotland must, unhappily, be for the moment regarded as rushing to the front with its new theology, which is no theology, but an opposition to the Word of the Lord. That church in which we all gloried, as sound in the faith and full of martyrs' spirit, has entrusted the training of its future ministers to two professors who hold other doctrines than those of its Confession. This is the most suicidal act a church could commit... Unless the whole church shall awake to its duty, the evangelicals in the Free Church are doomed to see another reign of moderatism.'[40]

What is clear, however, is that 'long before 1914' the views of Davidson, Smith, Bruce and Dods had 'triumphed in all the major Presbyterian churches of Scotland, and the biblical revolution had run its course'.[41] It is unspeakably sad from a conservative evangelical viewpoint that after Smeaton's death the liberal Marcus Dods (1834-1909) was elected to the New

Testament Chair at New College. As John Macleod curtly put it: 'Between the two men there was a yawning gulf.'[42]

Despite the efforts of Smeaton and fellow Free Church professors George C. M. Douglas (Glasgow) and William Binnie (Aberdeen), the critical views won the day in the Free Church. In James Robertson, professor of Oriental languages at Glasgow University, and W. L. Baxter, parish minister at Cameron in Fife, the Church of Scotland also had men who seriously challenged the critics.[43] The critical views, however, sadly were to dominate biblical scholarship through the twentieth century, and were unwittingly to devastate church life.

The critical movement of the late nineteenth century, as we have suggested, left a bitter legacy in the undermining of biblical orthodoxy and in confusion as to the authoritative basis of Christian faith and life. In the Free Church it arose in a very subtle way. Donald Maclean highlighted this in his Calvin Foundation lectures on 'Aspects of Scottish church history': 'A frank dualism is proposed in which a man can be a "traditionalist" and a "modernist" at the same time by the use of evangelical phraseology connoting entirely different conceptions from what a modernist actually believes. In this way they shall appear to hold evangelical beliefs while accepting modernist critical views.'[44]

The truth is that a church without an infallible, trustworthy and authoritative Bible will inevitably be a church in deep crisis facing declension. Downgrade in churches invariably arises from within rather than from without, something of which the church is clearly forewarned in the Lord's seven letters to the churches in Revelation chapters two and three and can well discern from the history of the churches which so readily adopted the critical views.

The Robertson Smith case was a watershed in Scottish church life. It was part and parcel of a terrible downgrade in biblical religion from the standpoint of the old orthodoxy. It was fearfully quick. And it grieved George Smeaton's heart. It showed the folly of moving ground on the subject of biblical inerrancy. Once that is conceded it will not be long before there is not much doctrine left. And when biblical doctrine is undermined it is not long before there is a shift in the moral principles. These things are tied up together. The integrity of biblical religion rests on a source which is utterly reliable and historically accurate. It is one of Smeaton's legacies to the church that he saw this connection in his day in the movements for change on the doctrine of Scripture in the church in the latter part of the nineteenth century.

In his interesting and helpful book on the ideas of the Free Church fathers on the inspiration of Scripture, Nicholas Needham counteracts the view that the seeds of the new liberalism were to be found, specifically, in germ in the thought of William Cunningham, James Bannerman and Robert Candlish. He demonstrates quite clearly that these men did hold to the plenary verbal inspiration and inerrancy of Scripture.[45] In this George Smeaton was at one with these men. It was fair to ask the question: How did it happen that the higher critical views so readily penetrated the Free Church? There is no easy answer to that. No doubt the reason is to be found in an undue willingness to concede ground to the anti-supernaturalism of the day which had received impetus from Darwinian evolutionary theories. In the course of the history of the Free Church, an increasing number of students studied in European faculties and imbibed ideas alien to the position of the early Free Church fathers, such as Smeaton. Doubtless the lesson is that there must be vigilance in the visible church to maintain with discipline and consistency the complete authority and absolute trustworthiness of the Scriptures as the only rule to direct us how we may glorify and enjoy God. There must surely be conscientiousness in maintaining truth and right in the church in this fallen world in which downgrade is a constant threat in the churches.

10.
Worship innovations

'My object is to show the
spirituality of the
Israelitish church as
evinced by its inspired and
invaluable Psalms. They
describe the eternity and
omnipresence, the majesty
and condescension, the
justice and mercy of
God...'

10.
Worship innovations

George Smeaton did not become involved in any direct way with the controversy over the expansion of praise in the Free Church beyond the Psalms. Discussions took place in the church from the mid-sixties, and in 1869 the committee on paraphrases and hymns reported to the General Assembly favourably to the introduction of 'human hymns'. Smeaton was not a member of that committee, though his colleague James MacGregor was. The systematic theology professor wrote a well-argued 'Memorial' to the 1869 General Assembly about the issue, in which he raised serious misgivings about the movement to introduce non-inspired materials of praise in to the Free Church.[1]

This was another matter that caused shock waves through the church. It was revolutionary, in that up till then only materials of divine inspiration had been used in congregational song, on the basis of the conservative, Calvinistic regulative principle that nothing should be admitted to the public worship of God which does not have express warrant from Scripture. This was based on a straightforward understanding of the first section of the twenty-first chapter of the *Westminster Confession of Faith*, which states: '…The acceptable way of worshipping the true God is instituted by himself, and so limited to his own revealed will, that he may not be worshipped according to the imaginations and devices of men, or the suggestions of Satan, under any visible representation, or any other way not prescribed in the holy Scripture.'

The formula to which the ministers subscribed was also perfectly clear. They vowed to 'own the purity of worship

presently authorized and practised in the Free Church of
Scotland', which practice was accepted as being 'founded on
the Word of God, and agreeable thereto'. All students apply-
ing to be received as ministers, and such men being subsequently ordained into a pastoral charge, were required to
assert, maintain and defend the said worship and follow no
divisive course from it. What was being proposed in the
introduction of uninspired hymns and instrumental accompaniment was, however, a significant departure from the previously authorized practices considered to be 'agreeable to the
Word'.

Men such as James Begg, James Gibson[2] and Hugh Martin,[3] along with William Balfour of Holyrood Free Church and
many others, were concerned over the issue. They were in the
forefront of opposition to the move. However, a collection of
Psalms and paraphrases with a selection of hymns was
approved by the Free Church General Assembly of 1872. The
legislation was of a permissive nature and so the use of the
hymns was patchy and in some areas there was strong
resistance to the use of hymns. A *Free Church Hymn Book*
was produced for the first time in 1882. This gave impetus to
the hymns movement in the Free Church.

In Smeaton's own congregation there was a move to introduce the *Free Church Hymn Book* in 1883. Horatius
Bonar (1808-89) was the minister of that congregation,
Chalmers' Memorial Free Church, Grange. He had a real
poetical gift and was the writer of many highly regarded
evangelical hymns. The question of the use in public worship
of the 1882 book, which contained many of Bonar's hymns,
came up in the congregation in 1883. Smeaton was an elder
in that congregation. Another elder at the Grange was William
Nixon (1803-1900), who had retired as minister in Montrose
in 1874. He had been popularly known as 'The Lion of
Montrose' and was among the most prominent of the constitutionalists in the Free Church. When the matter was forced,
by Bonar and other elders in the autumn of 1883, Smeaton,

Nixon and six other elders (out of a total of twenty-one) issued a statement on the proposal, indicating that they were not prepared to sanction the use of the *Free Church Hymn Book* in congregational worship. This was essentially on grounds of principle, but also embraced the practical consideration that the move would cause conflict and create disharmony within the congregation. The majority of the Kirk Session, however, went ahead with the proposal to introduce the hymn book. As a consequence George Smeaton, with others, resigned from the eldership of the congregation he had been instrumental in planting twenty years earlier.[4] The issue created quite a stir and was reported in *The Signal* magazine of 1 May 1884.

As far as Smeaton's own opinions are concerned, the only thing really bearing on this question is found in his *Doctrine of the Holy Spirit* (1889), where we read these significant words in relation to the Psalms:

> ...The Psalms to which we are adverting, when considered as the actual expression of praise for the Israelitish church, as well as a legacy handed down to us in the Christian church, sufficiently refute that view. No book of a similar kind was prepared for the New Testament church. The Holy Spirit, replenishing the sweet singers of Israel with spiritual truth and holy love, anticipated in this way much of the necessity that should be felt in Christian times. I am not here discussing the important, though still debated, point as to the use of Psalms in public worship. My object is to show the spirituality of the Israelitish church as evinced by its inspired and invaluable Psalms. They describe the eternity and omnipresence, the majesty and condescension, the justice and mercy of God in a strain of the most fervid devotion. They sing of repentance and faith, of joy in God and delight in God's law, with an ardour beyond which it is impossible to go. They depict Christ's royal reign

and his union with his church; the anointing with the oil of gladness (Ps. 45:7); the receiving of gifts for men (Ps. 68:18); and the supreme dominion with which Christ was to be invested by the Father with a tenderness, unction, and joy, to which no other words are equal. And those Psalms which are called 'new songs' anticipate the full millennial glory.[5]

Smeaton was also clearly unhappy about the permissive allowance of instrumental music for the accompaniment of praise in the Free Church after 1883. He wrote a preface to a pamphlet by the Rev. John M'Ewan (1826-1907) arguing against such an innovation.[6] In this preface he points out that Voetius made an 'unanswerable' argument against instruments in public worship in his *Politica Ecclesiastica* (1663).[7] Smeaton concurs with these arguments against the adoption of instrumental music. He says: 'I deplore the disturbance of the unity, peace and spiritual prosperity of the church by the introduction of new elements in worship, which are not in keeping with the genius of Scottish Presbyterianism. I trust that all wise men will do what in them lies to guard the church from such experiments as these. The truth is, that organs and organ recitals, artistic execution and fine performances, are vain appliances, and do not touch the real disease. Enlightened Christians know what is a-wanting, and what alone will take off the load from the heavy heart. Certainly instrumental music will not yield that result.'[8]

This is another area in which there were significant changes in practices in the course of the century. Up to the latter part of the nineteenth century, there was widespread acceptance of the general Calvinistic principle, so succinctly stated in the *Westminster Confession of Faith*, that nothing should be admitted to the worship of God except what is warranted by the Word of God or what by good and necessary consequence may be deduced from the Word. This principle was well stated by William Cunningham in an article

in *The British and Foreign Evangelical Review* of April 1860:
'The Calvinistic section of the Reformers, following their great
master, adopted a stricter rule, and were of opinion, that
there were sufficiently plain indications in Scripture itself, that
it was Christ's mind and will, that nothing should be introduced into the government and worship of the church, unless
a positive warrant for it could be found in Scripture. This
principle was adopted and acted upon by the English Puritans
and the Scottish Presbyterians; and we are persuaded that it is
the only true and safe principle applicable to this matter.'[9]

In the Presbyterian churches in Scotland in the course of
the nineteenth century there was, however, a distinct breach
with the Puritan practice that had previously prevailed. A
radical change in worship was given impetus by the cam-
paigns of American evangelists Dwight L. Moody and Ira D.
Sankey, who visited Edinburgh for the first time in November
1873. This led to unhappy but inevitable controversy among
friends, as John Kennedy of Dingwall, with whom Smeaton
would clearly have sympathized in this matter, took issue with
Horatius Bonar in relation to the influences of the work of
Moody and Sankey in Scotland.[10]

It was felt by Kennedy that the methods adopted by the
American evangelists did much to undermine the erstwhile
conservative principle and practice of the Presbyterian
church. Although the practice of exclusive unaccompanied
psalmody in public worship is very much a minority position
nowadays, it is interesting that the whole matter is still debated.[11] It is also clear that once a church adopts a regulative
principle which allows what is not specifically 'forbidden' by
the Word of God, this tends to open the door to all sorts of
innovations which invariably causes disuniformity and divi-
siveness in the church, or among churches.

At any rate such issues caused George Smeaton sadness
as he came towards the end of his days and saw so many
shifts in the position of the Free Church, both in doctrine and
in practice. It was for these reasons that Smeaton moved from

the Grange to the congregation of Buccleuch Free Church on West Crosscauseway, where he felt more comfortable with the form of worship and happily sat under the ministry of Robert Gordon, son of one of the most prominent Disruption ministers of the same name.[12] This was a sad chapter in the lives of the Smeatons.

11.
Inspiration

'To make the Bible merely a literary work, however historically accurate, forfeits all appeal to it as the court of last resort, and only opens the floodgates of uncertainty and error.'

11.

Inspiration

The enduring legacy of George Smeaton lies in his writings on the atonement and the Holy Spirit, and on his contributions on the subject of national Christianity. He wrote some effective controversial pamphlets, especially on the question of church union and the Establishment Principle. But without question the strength of Smeaton's writings lay in the fact that they were such positive statements of truth. His finest works, on the atonement and the Holy Spirit, have become classics of Reformed theology. The style of his writing is not as laboured as that of his colleague, William Cunningham. John Macleod comments that, 'Dr Smeaton was the master of a very clear and unobtrusive style of expression.'[1] His major volumes are not so taken up with the passing controversies of the day, such as the books of James Begg, for example, which scarcely lent themselves to be reprinted in later years.

Apart from an early publication of a discourse on 'Immanuel' in *The Scottish Christian Herald* of 1840, and the publication of lectures on 'Necessary harmony between doctrine and spiritual life' (1853) and 'The basis of Christian doctrine in divine fact' (1854), most of Smeaton's writings were produced in his more mature years, after 1868. He was fifty-four years old when his first volume, *The Doctrine of the Atonement as Taught by Christ Himself*, appeared in 1868. The second volume, *The Doctrine of the Atonement as Taught by the Apostles*, came out two years later. In between times, he was asked to write a biography of an outstanding layman whom he had known in Aberdeen days, *Memoir of Alexander Thomson of Banchory* (1869). Smeaton's desire was that his subject 'appears in this memoir as he thought

and spoke and acted among his fellows'.[2] The volume comprises an interesting social commentary on the period of the
subject's life (1798-1868) and capably weaves together historical and spiritual factors in Thomson's life largely from writings
and letters.

Before considering George Smeaton's contribution to exegetical theology in his works on the atonement and the Holy
Spirit, it is important to recognize the whole basis of his position in relation to revelation and inspiration. He lived through a
period in which there was increasing downgrade from the
theology of the Westminster standards and the high doctrine of
Scripture upon which it was based. What was Smeaton's
position on Scripture? It is quite clear that from first to last
George Smeaton held a high view of the divine inspiration of
Holy Scripture as an infallible record of divine revelation.

In his 1854 lecture in the Aberdeen College on the 'Basis of
Christian doctrine in divine fact', he makes this clear statement:
'...It must be evident at a glance that we must have a perfect
medium of revelation, free from error and from the slightest
tincture of mistake, if we have an accurately drawn portraiture
of the personal Redeemer. A compromise in inspiration is
fatal.'[3] Christian revelation is both fact-based and book-based,
maintains Smeaton: 'The Word ... as the self-manifestation of
the Redeemer, and as the channel for communicating all his
fullness, must be perfect.' What was then coming out of Germany, however, in making light of the supernatural basis of
Christianity, 'is like a bleeding wound, nay a death-wound in
the bosom of the very development which they have given
us'.[4] Right to the end he maintained that, 'The Scriptures,
inspired by the Holy Spirit, are the court of last appeal to every
religious mind and to every Christian church for the defence of
truth and for the refutation of error.'[5]

It is clear that by the late 1870s Smeaton was aware that
there was a shift in the churches on the doctrine of Scripture.
He recognized, as we have seen, that the higher critical
theories were incompatible with the dogma of an infallible

Bible. In 1879 he was responsible for re-issuing a 'chapter
from Thomas Chalmers', as he called it, 'On the inspiration of
the Old and New Testaments'. It is clear that he wished to
remind the Free Church of its roots in relation to the infallibility of Scripture, not least in its full trustworthiness in historical
facts but also as an inspired and infallible Book. In his introduction to the work of Chalmers, Smeaton attacks the 'mediating theology' of Friedrich Schleiermacher and other German writers, 'which allows a revelation in historic facts, but
denies the biblical or book-revelation in any true acceptation
of the term. Revelation is restricted by them to the divine facts
and words of the personal Redeemer but disjoined from any
accompanying inspiration on the mind of those who composed the records. In a word, the historical revelation is
isolated from the book-revelation.' The consequence? 'All this
leads, by natural consequence, to a treatment of the Bible
akin to that which a petulant modern reviewer metes out to a
new literary production. Divine authority there is none in the
book as such; certainty is at an end; conjecture reigns para-
mount; mental autonomy under law to none has chartered
licence.'[6] This is very much to the point in relation to the
divine inspiration of Scripture.

Smeaton takes up this notion of the autonomy of the human mind reigning supreme in biblical criticism in his later
volume, *The Doctrine of the Holy Spirit*. It is clear by comparing the first edition of this work (1882) with the second, completed just a few weeks before his death (1889), that George
Smeaton is constrained in the later edition to expand the
material on the question of the full inspiration of Scripture. To
his third lecture he adds in the 1889 edition some material
relating to what he calls 'the great and far-reaching questions
raised among us', namely, 'Are we to take Scripture as a
supernatural production of the Holy Spirit? And are we to
believe on the AUTHORITY of Scripture as a revelation?'[7]
Smeaton expresses his deep concern: 'The attempt made
during this generation to sunder the revelation of historic fact

from the biblical revelation, and to treat the Bible as a literary
work alone, apart from every other consideration, is the most
marked feature of modern thought, and the ground on which
the so-called autonomy of the human mind claims to be
emancipated from outward control. That is the source', he
maintains, 'of all the great conflicts of our time, and the breach
in the embankment through which the tide of error is sweeping
in.'[8]

Smeaton proceeds to address the question of 'The work of
the Spirit in the inspiration of prophets and apostles' in an
entirely orthodox way.[9] The prophets and apostles were
supernaturally gifted. The apostles were special organs of
Christ's revelation to the church: '*The Holy Spirit supplied
prophets and apostles, as chosen organs, with gifts which
must be distinguished from ordinary grace, to give forth in
human forms of speech a revelation which must be accepted
as the word of God in its whole contents, and as the authoritative guide for doctrine and duty.*'[10] Smeaton is surely right
when he affirms that, 'The reception of the Spirit's supernatural inspiration lays the foundation for ALL THE AUTHORITY
of revelation. Revelation is accepted and obeyed, not on the
ground of its adaptation to my reason or conscience —
though it is in harmony with both — but on the ground of its
supernatural and theopneustic [i.e. inspired, God-breathed]
character.'[11] He goes on to say, 'It is this faith of authority that
has given rise to all the achievements, devotional ardour, and
martyr zeal of the Christian church.'[12] Smeaton's position may
be summarized in this way: The Holy Spirit testifies only
through Scripture and not apart from it; and the reception of
the supernatural inspiration of the Holy Spirit lays the foundation for all the authority of revelation.

Smeaton's concern about this doctrine in the wake of the
Robertson Smith case is evident in an additional section in
the survey of the history of the doctrine of the Spirit, included
in the second edition of his work on the Holy Spirit.[13] Under
the heading 'Inspiration of the Spirit as at present discussed',

he opens his discussion with the statement that, 'The inadequate views of many on the supernatural action of the Spirit comes to light in the current opinions on the origin and authority of Scripture.'[14] He then goes on to affirm, 'That the whole Word of God was composed by the inspiration of the Spirit, and that holy men selected as organs of revelation spoke as they were moved by the Holy Ghost (2 Peter 1:21), has been always held in the church is an undoubted axiom.'[15]

Norman Madsen, in his 1974 thesis on Smeaton, characterizes the latter's view of revelation in this way: 'Smeaton maintains the direct and absolute self-revelation of God through the Scripture record. He was so concerned not to allow the holy Scripture to be seen as simply a human document or even a "human document of a revelation ... the literary work of men", that he rejected outright any possible justification for higher criticism of the Scriptures.'[16]

In this quotation Madsen cites Smeaton's work on the Holy Spirit, the fuller quotation of which reads: '...A compromise or concession on the authority of Scripture, or, which amounts to the same thing, an admission that it is but the human document of a revelation, and that the Bible is nothing more than the literary work of men, carries with it consequences the most disastrous. To make the Bible merely a literary work, however historically accurate, forfeits all appeal to it as the court of last resort, and only opens the floodgates of uncertainty and error.' To this Smeaton adds: 'A surrender of biblical revelation is fatal.'[17] This high view of revelation characterizes all of Smeaton's writings.

There is very little to indicate what interest George Smeaton took in matters of textual criticism. But he lived in the era of the Revised Version translation[18] and the theories of B. F. Westcott and F. J. A. Hort,[19] which every bit as much as the higher critical theories constituted a sharp departure from the previously held consensus in the Reformed churches in these areas. It is perhaps of interest that Smeaton, such a recognized Greek scholar, took no part in the committee brought

together to produce a Revised Version, though his corresponding colleague in the Aberdeen College, David Brown,
became a member of that committee.

Though only suggestive of his attitude, it is perhaps significant that in a comment on Luke 1:35 in his work on the Holy
Spirit, he challenges the Revised Version translation.[20] In the
same work, with a reference to Luke 2:40, Smeaton follows the
textus receptus reading behind the Authorized Version translation: 'And the child grew and waxed strong in Spirit (πνεύματι),
filled with wisdom.' In a footnote (in both editions of his work)
he says: 'This reading has a predominance of authority in its
favour.'[21] Before the modern textual theories and apparatus
prevailed, this was the received opinion in line with the majority of Greek manuscripts. Smeaton in one place also quotes
with approval Dean John William Burgon's support of the
genuineness of the phrase 'the Son of man who is in heaven'
from John 3:13.[22] Smeaton notably does not use the Revised
Version in the 1889 edition of his work on the Holy Spirit. It
appears that he took a conservative line on matters of textual
criticism, as he most certainly did on the question of the higher
criticism and the inspiration and authority of the Scriptures.

To Smeaton the matter of divine inspiration and the authority of Scripture were inextricably linked. There could not be the
authority without the inspiration and infallibility of Scripture. A
low view of inspiration 'runs counter to the presence of the
Spirit in any sense, and to the divine authority of the Scripture
in any sense'.[23] In this regard Smeaton was a prophetic voice in
his own day. His fears concerning a low view of inspiration
were fully justified. Such a low view has spawned marked
declension in the church, accompanied as it has been with a
lack of power. Smeaton saw the connection: 'As to the bold
criticism of Scripture, proceeding as it does on a denial of its
inspiration by the Spirit, it has no significance and no attrac-
tions for the mind that has personally come under the supernatural and regenerating operations of the Spirit.'[24]

12.
The atonement

'The doctrine of the atonement is put in its proper light only when it is regarded as the central truth of Christianity and the great theme of Scripture.'

12.
The atonement

George Smeaton put the whole matter of the atonement of Christ in perspective in the opening sentence of his first volume on the subject: 'The doctrine of the atonement is put in its proper light only when it is regarded as the central truth of Christianity and the great theme of Scripture.'[1]

In both his volumes on the atonement, the author's aim was to survey the entire New Testament teaching on the subject. The works are therefore exegetical and expository rather than dogmatic. 'I have endeavoured', he says in one place, 'to bring out the results of exegetical investigation, not the process, and to put these within the reach of the educated English reader, to aid him in the great work of making himself acquainted with the Lord's mind, through the medium of the language of revelation.'[2] He emphasizes this later: 'Our plan leads us to proceed in an exegetical way, and not to argue from general principles or from mere dogmatic grounds, except as the discussion of the words of our Lord conducts us to the confines of that field.'[3]

In his preface to the second volume, Smeaton states, 'The work is rather biblical than formally dogmatic or polemical, and intended to embody positive truth according to the setting in which the doctrine is placed in the apostolic documents.'[4] Smeaton explains his approach explicitly in this way: 'The object steadily kept in view has been to determine what saith the Scripture — according to rigid principles of grammatico-historical interpretation — without dislocating or wresting, so far as I am aware, a single expression from its true significance, and thus to run up the matter of authority. Then only do we listen to the word of God, and not to the speculations or wisdom of men.'[5] He states in the same volume, in relation to a particular application of this principle, that, 'The rules of sound interpretation require not only that we shall examine the import of the terms, but the passages where they are found, the connection of the context, and the appended words which put the ransom and deliverance in the relation of cause and effect.'[6]

Smeaton's work was ground-breaking. It is to be seriously doubted that the magnitude of his achievement in these volumes on the atonement, and especially in the first, was really appreciated in his own day. They are possibly the most outstanding works of biblical theology and exegesis to appear from the nineteenth-century Scottish church. In passage after passage Smeaton effectively drives home the biblical truth in relation to the death of Christ, demonstrating that it constituted vicarious penal satisfaction. His work stands as a serious challenge to all other 'theories' of the atonement. In that respect his work remains fresh and persuasive to this day. This much is recognized by later scholars. Goddard, for example, said this in 1953: 'It is important to point out that these two volumes give a comprehensive treatment of the doctrine, and furnish a complete source book on all atonement passages in the New Testament Scriptures. Here is a very complete analysis of the teachings of Jesus on this vital subject. Most of Smeaton's philological work substantially justifies his position on the doctrine, and is therefore a great source of strength to those who believe and teach as he does.'[7]

The volumes are arranged somewhat differently. The second edition of the first volume, on *Christ's Doctrine of the Atonement*, has fifty-two sections spread among eight chapters, each of which opens up various aspects of the death of Christ as unfolded in the gospels.[8] The approach is thematic rather than consecutive. Besides the careful examinations of all the sayings of Christ in relation to his atoning work, there is also an enormously useful appendix on 'Notes and historical elucidations'.[9] These notes give an effective glimpse into Smeaton's immense learning.

In both volumes, however, Smeaton is especially concerned that the truths expounded should be accessible to 'the educated English reader', and so the reader is not overburdened by the appearances of scholarship. In that respect Smeaton retains a 'light touch', something that has made the books attractive for a wide readership and not just a scholarly community.

The second volume, on *The Apostles' Doctrine of the Atonement*, surveys the apostolic testimony in connection with the atoning work of the Lord. Smeaton does this by consecutively studying all the references to the atonement outside the gospels. The arrangement is not quite so helpful as the first volume in that the section headings do not set out the material in terms of theological categories. Smeaton, however, deals with all the relevant passages consecutively and with great thoroughness and skill. The second volume is also a sound, masterly and stimulating work.

The volumes are clearly the result of mature reflection and ripe scholarship. Smeaton believed that the atonement was central to the entire Christian faith and to any adequate understanding of the Bible. The only revealed purpose of the incarnation, to Smeaton, is the atonement. He holds to the understanding of Christ's death as one of penal satisfaction, or substitution. 'Jesus was visited', he says, 'with penal suffering, because he appeared before God only in the guise of our accumulated sin; not therefore as a private individual, but as a representative; sinless in himself, but sin-covered; loved as a Son, but condemned as a sin-bearer, in virtue of that federal union between him and his people, which lay at the foundation of the whole. Thus God condemned sin in the flesh, and in consequence of this there is no condemnation to us.'[10]

To Smeaton, the atonement was necessary to avert punishment: 'There could be no other reason sufficiently important for God to abase himself and to be made in fashion as a man, and suffer on the cross; for God would not subject his

Son to such agonies if sin could have been remitted without satisfaction.'[11] The source of the atonement is God himself.

In regard to John 3:16, Smeaton says, 'The atonement is here described as emanating from the love of God.'[12] He adds, rhetorically, 'If love is in proportion to the difficulties to be overcome, and if redemption could be effected only at the cost of the humiliation and crucifixion of the Son of God, the love which did not allow itself to be deterred by such a sacrifice was infinite. Then only does love fully come to light; and they who do not acknowledge the necessity of the satisfaction can have no adequate conception of love.'[13]

In the first serious assessment of George Smeaton's theology, Homer Lehr Goddard, while he has a profound appreciation of the exegetical and theological competence of the man, criticizes him on several counts in relation to the works on the atonement. Goddard sees a deficiency in what he considers on Smeaton's part a 'minimizing [of] the active participation of God the Father in the redemption of man from the curse and power of sin'.[14] He finds it difficult to see how the vicarious punishment inflicted by the Father on the Son can be squared with the overwhelming love of God as the source of redemption and reconciliation. Goddard suggests that this deficiency would have been resolved if Smeaton had 'perceived as truth or suggested that God in Christ suffered to conquer and take away sin, and reconcile man to himself'.[15]

Smeaton, however, does stress the divine love providing the atonement in dealing with John 3:16.[16] He reflects very clearly the biblical teaching that it was the *God-man* who suffered. That is the point in relation to the necessity for the incarnation for the provision of the atonement — it is not the Father who suffers, it is the incarnate Son who suffers, according to the demands of divine justice in relation to sin and its punishment. Furthermore, it is the God-man who suffers in his human nature. For, 'The divine nature did not suffer, and could not; but in virtue of its union to the humanity, the latter was able to encounter and to bear more than mere man could have borne, because it was supported and strengthened for that end.'[17] But it was certainly divine love that made such a provision, through the offering up of God's Son to accomplish redemption for sinners. In relation to the sending of Jesus by the Father, Smeaton says that, 'The sending is thus an expression of authority, and a manifestation of every divine attribute working together to a definite object. But it is specially an exhibition of *unmerited love or grace*. The atonement emanated from sovereign grace, and was an expression of the boundless and incomprehensible love of God's heart to sinful men.'[18]

Goddard also considers that Smeaton fails to recognize the place of the resurrection in gospel preaching,[19] that he seemed to ignore the tremendous significance of the resurrection as it validated the atonement.[20] However, Smeaton does have a section in his first volume in which he clearly spells out the connection between the Lord's atonement and his resurrection.[21] He goes as far as to say this: 'The Lord's resurrection, the Christian's boast, the pledge of all our hope, is in a special sense the foundation of our religion.'[22] In a comment on the Letter to the Hebrews, chapter nine, in his second volume on the atonement, Smeaton says this: 'If we want proof that the atonement was accepted, and procured forgiveness of sins, this was proved by the Lord's resurrection from the dead, corresponding as it did to the coming out of the high priest from the holiest of all to give the priestly benediction to the people.'[23] However, 'The resurrection of the Lord does not enter into the meritorious part of the Redeemer's work, that is, into the element which divines call the impetration of redemption.'[24] How are they related, the atonement and the resurrection? 'The atonement and resurrection stand to each other in relation of service and reward, of cause and effect.'[25]

As far as the extent of the atonement is concerned, Smeaton expounds the classic Calvinistic doctrine of limited or definite atonement: 'The purchase of redemption and its application are co-extensive. The salvation is not won for any for whom it is not applied: the Christ will not lose one for whom he died. To suppose the opposite would imply that a costly price had been paid, and that those for whom it was paid derived no advantage from it; which could only be on the ground that he wanted either love or power. Not only so: a concurrent action and perfect harmony must be supposed to obtain among the three persons of the Godhead. There can be no disharmony between the election of the Father, the redemption of the Son, and the application of the Spirit.'[26] As to the question of how the special atonement may be harmonized with the general invitation of the gospel to mankind indiscriminately, Smeaton says this: 'That the offer of salvation is to be made to all men is the conclusion to which every one must come who duly considers that Christ so preached... A special atonement and invitations sincerely made on the ground of it to mankind indefinitely, are quite compatible.'[27]

There is of course an absolute necessity for faith in receiving the benefits of Christ's death. Says Smeaton, with reference to John 6:32-53: 'Faith is thus the appointed means, and the only means, by which any man can enjoy the saving efficacy of Christ's atoning death; and no words could more forcibly point out the indispensable necessity of faith for a participation in the saving efficacy of Christ's atoning sacrifice. This is the one means of reception. He who believes receives the saving blessings which Christ's death procured, and has a right to the fulfilment of the promise. He who receives with the heart the gift of the crucified Christ, has a right to pardon, and can claim it.'[28]

It goes without saying that the possession or otherwise of faith in the atoning blood of Jesus is crucial to the eternal destiny of the entirety of mankind. In his final chapter in the first volume on the atonement, Smeaton deals with 'the endless happiness or woe of mankind decided by the reception or rejection of the atonement'.[29] With reference to Matthew 25:46, Smeaton says that this 'awful truth' is brought out 'when our Lord speaks of *everlasting* punishment, using

the same word with which he speaks of life'. Any argument
that a different meaning may be given to the word in these
instances 'would be to violate all the rules of just interpretation'. 'It remains', says Smeaton, 'that the same word is
equally applied to the heavenly blessedness and to the future
misery; and on no principle of interpretation can an expositor
be allowed to give a different sense to the same word in two
contrasted clauses.'[30] This theme Smeaton describes as 'awful
in the extreme, and one which no one can approach without
a bleeding heart'. The frequency with which the Lord refers to
the theme is, says Smeaton, 'a merciful forewarning, intended
to shut men up to the all-sufficient atonement'.[31]

The fact that Smeaton provided in these volumes such an
orthodox exposition of the biblical doctrine of the atonement
sadly did not endear the books to Smeaton's contemporaries.
In his biography of Donald John Martin, Norman C.
Macfarlane says that 'Older men kept on their shelves his [i.e.
Smeaton's] books on the atonement and his Cunningham
Lectures on the Holy Spirit, but the younger men gave them
no place.'[32] The truth is that these volumes of Smeaton are
still highly valued and appreciated to this day by all who love
the Reformed faith. They are all still in print, whereas the sort
of books which the 'younger men' of Donald John Martin's
day so revered have dropped into notable and arguably
deserved obscurity.

The first volume on the atonement went into a second edition in 1871, some forty pages longer than the first edition.
The title of the volume on the spine of the second edition is
printed as *Our Lord's Doctrine of the Atonement*. 'It ought
not to be overlooked', said Malcolm Kinnear in his 1995
thesis on 'Scottish New Testament scholarship and the
atonement c.1845-1920', 'that Smeaton's two books were the
first comprehensive, scholarly exegetical analysis of the New
Testament teaching on the atonement from a British author in
this period, and in thoroughness and detail his work has not
been paralleled since in the English language. Smeaton was a

learned man of deep religious insight, and this will not go unnoticed by careful readers of his work.'[33]

Kinnear goes on to say this: 'Smeaton was the first professional biblical scholar to take up the issue of the atonement, and his exegetical focus anticipated the character of later discussions. His work was detailed and thorough. His scholarly method was, on the whole, reasonably balanced between the need to examine the background of a difficult word and the actual New Testament usage and context as a means of pinpointing its meaning.'[34]

A successor to George Smeaton in the Chair of New Testament in New College, John O'Neill, has commented that Smeaton's criticism of those who broke loose from previous conclusions of the doctrine of the atonement 'was based on thorough knowledge of what those conclusions were'.[35] He quotes a comment of Smeaton's which provides an excellent summary of Smeaton's overall view of the atoning work of Christ: 'That which places the church upon Bible Christianity, and severs her from every phase of rationalism, is the firm belief that the atonement was the work of the incarnate Son, and that it is a provision offered by the divine love for the satisfaction of the inflexible claims of divine holiness and justice.'[36]

By his thorough exegetical approach to all the New Testament references to the atoning work of Christ, Smeaton drives home the truth that it was a penal satisfaction and substitution, absolutely necessary for the salvation of all who by grace come to faith in him. The cumulative argument is irresistible, and Smeaton's work retains a persuasive freshness on the whole matter of the meaning and accomplishment of Christ's sacrificial death for sinners.

Dr Roger Nicole, then of Gordon Divinity School in the USA, wrote about Smeaton's work on the atonement that it 'represents a very thorough study of the whole New Testament evidence bearing on this cardinal doctrine. Smeaton was a very careful scholar thoroughly steeped in the Reformed faith ... of profound faith, comprehensive scholarship and exceptional clarity of expression and insight... Every conservative man should consider it a privilege to possess such valuable material...'[37]

There is in these volumes a wonderful resource for preachers in sermon preparation of exegetical material on all the New Testament texts bearing on the grand and central theme of the atoning work of the incarnate Saviour.

13.
The Holy Spirit

It was Smeaton's aim to ... keep before men's minds and hearts the great Scripture truths concerning the personality and work of the Holy Spirit.

13.
The Holy Spirit

The Cunningham Lectureship was the consequence of a trust set up by a prominent Free Church elder, William Binny Webster, in 1862. It was founded in memory of Principal William Cunningham, the foremost Free Church theologian of his day, who had died in 1861. The purpose of the lectureship arose from the founder's desire for the 'success of the Free Church College, Edinburgh', and the advance of 'the theological literature of Scotland'. Lecturers were appointed for two years and were entitled to the income of the endowment. The endowment was £2,000 and the annual income around £120, considerable sums for those days. The lecturer was at liberty to choose his own subject. There were to be at least six lectures, and the lecturers — at their own risk — were to print and publish no fewer than 750 copies of the lectures.

George Smeaton was the ninth lecturer under the trust. His subject was the doctrine of the Holy Spirit, and the lectures were delivered in New College during 1882. Duly printed and published that year by T. & T. Clark, the work comprised three 'divisions'. The first was introductory, dealing with the doctrine of the Trinity and the biblical testimony concerning the work of the Spirit. The second division comprised six lectures dealing with the positive doctrinal or dogmatic truth concerning the work of the Spirit. In a third division, Smeaton gives an historical survey of the doctrine of the Holy Spirit from the apostolic age.

It has to be said that he appears to be in his element both with this important subject in general, and especially with his historical surveys, in this connection and also in connection with that on the work of the atonement. He was a master in the field of historical theology, matched in the nineteenth century, arguably, only by William Cunningham. In the first published edition, the work comprises 372 pages. By the time he came to complete the second edition in 1889, shortly before his death, the work was considerably extended, particularly, as we have indicated previously, in the area of the work of the Holy Spirit in connection with the inspiration of the holy Scriptures, an issue clearly deepening in importance for Smeaton.[1]

Again, this work was warmly received by all lovers of the truth. The work must stand as one of the finest ever produced on the subject. Dr A. A. Hodge, in a review for *The Presbyterian Review* of April 1883, said that it 'probably surpasses in value all that has proceeded from the same author. The entire work is biblical, doctrinal, historical, and eminently sound and learned'.[2]

Interestingly, Hodge does take up one issue with the book. He describes as 'unprofitable and unbecoming', the speculation that in the constitution of the theanthropic person of Christ,[3] 'The communication from the one nature to the other was by the Spirit, the executive of all the works of God.' (The quotation is found on page 126 of the 1882 edition.)

Smeaton makes a similar and beautiful statement elsewhere, in commenting on the clause in Hebrews 9:14, 'who through the eternal Spirit offered himself without spot to God': 'The Holy Spirit was the executive of all Christ's actions, internal and external; and those actions, peculiarly fragrant because of their spirituality, derived their worth, so far as intrinsic merit was concerned, from the fact that they were the actions of the Son. The meaning of the clause under consideration is that the Holy Ghost, filling the Lord's humanity with unspeakable compassion, ardent zeal, fortitude, energy and fervent love, impelled him forward on his atoning work, and never suffered his mind to cool till the sacrifice was accomplished.'[4]

It is interesting that Smeaton, obviously aware of Hodge's criticism, adds in the 1889 second edition, by way of explanation, a lengthy quotation from a sermon of a Bishop Horsley in justification of his position, which he retains unaltered. (It is on page 134 of the second edition of the work.)[5]

Though Smeaton's point is arguably speculative, what he says is very much in line with, for example, the position of the Puritan John Owen, who in one place says this with regard to the relation of the Holy Spirit to the human nature of Christ: 'The Holy Spirit is the Spirit of the Son, no less than the Spirit of the Father. He proceedeth from the Son, as from the Father. He is the "Spirit of the Son" (Gal. 4:6). And hence is he the immediate operator of all divine acts of the Son himself, even on his own human nature. Whatever the Son of God wrought in, by, or upon the human nature, he did it by the Holy Ghost, who is his Spirit, as he is the Spirit of the Father.'[6]

Owen states in similar vein later in relation to the person of Christ that, 'All the voluntary communications of the divine nature unto the human were, as we have showed, by the Holy Spirit.'[7] Robert Shillaker helpfully deals with this issue in a part of his thesis on 'The federal pneumatology of George Smeaton' in which he takes issue with Hodge's criticism. In order to resolve the issue as to how the two natures of Christ will neither be confused or mixed, nor divided or separated in the life and work of the Redeemer, it is entirely plausible to hold that this will be accomplished through the work of the third person of the Trinity co-operatively upon and within the God-man. As Shillaker puts it: 'While Smeaton's views display an advance in detail over many Reformed Christological explanations, they are not totally unique, nor is it an unreasonable attempt to explain how the incarnate Christ (as understood in Reformed Christology) can function.'[8]

Smeaton's thinking behind the volume is clear. He says: 'Except where Puritan influences are still at work, we may safely affirm that the doctrine of the Spirit is almost entirely

ignored. The representatives of modern theology, it is well
known, have almost wholly abandoned it.'[9] It was Smeaton's
aim to make good this deficiency and keep before men's
minds and hearts the great Scripture truths concerning the
personality and work of the Holy Spirit: 'The distinctive
feature of Christianity, as it addresses itself to man's experience, is the work of the Spirit, which not only elevates it far
above all philosophical speculation, but also above every
other form of religion.'[10]

In an article entitled 'Recent dogmatic thought in Scotland'
in *The Presbyterian and Reformed Review* of April 1891,
Principal John Cairns (1818-92) of the United Presbyterian
Hall in Edinburgh described this book of Smeaton's as, 'one
of the ablest works ever written on the Holy Spirit'.[11] More
recently, in *A Reader's Guide to Reformed Literature*, produced in 1999, Dr Joel R. Beeke says this with reference to
the Holy Spirit: 'Begin with George Smeaton. His work on the
Spirit is readable, thorough, and edifying.'[12]

In his 1974 thesis on the theology of George Smeaton,
Norman Madsen brings out the relationship in Smeaton's
thinking between the atonement and the work of the Holy
Spirit. He comments, 'Smeaton's works on the doctrine of the
atonement and the doctrine of the Holy Spirit are of interest
not only because of their dogmatic presentation of these two
doctrines but more importantly because of the way he sys-
tematically thinks through the relation between atonement
and pneumatology based upon the conjoint revelatory activity
of the Son and the Spirit.'[13]

Among the issues that Smeaton addresses is the matter of
the cessation of the special gifts of the apostolic age — the
special 'charismatic' gifts. He distinguishes between the
extraordinary gifts and the 'gifts of an ordinary character':
'The rich supply of the *extraordinary gifts* bestowed at Pentecost was not intended to continue when they had served their
purpose in founding the Christian church. The other *gifts of*

an ordinary character were given for the permanent advantage of the church.'[14]

These ordinary gifts are essential to the edification of the
church, and without them it would collapse. Some of them,
avers Smeaton, are 'gifts of office' for acting on the minds of
others, 'while the general body of Christians are supplied with
the gifts and endowments, wealth and influence which the
Spirit induces them to wield for the common benefit.'[15]

Notwithstanding his cessationist position in the matter of
extraordinary gifts (tongues, healings, revelations), Smeaton is
not hesitant to speak about the necessity of a pouring out of
the Spirit in every age, as we have seen from his earlier
sermon, 'A witnessing church — a church baptized with the
Holy Ghost'.[16] As a man who had experienced this in Disruption days, and subsequent awakenings in 1859-60, he had
seen just such a work of the Spirit. Smeaton does say that the
work of the Spirit 'wherever it occurs, requires to be discrimi-
nated from its accompaniments and from the counterfeits that
may be expected',[17] for, 'Where the Spirit builds a church,
Satan builds a chapel.'[18] There will always be tares among the
wheat, but where a soul passes through deep conviction to
triumphant faith, and when there is perceptible deliverance
from errors previously held, and of course where there is
continuance in the life of faith, then there must be a presump-
tion of a genuine work.

It is fitting that George Smeaton ends his great work on the
Holy Spirit with a practical section, 'Be filled with the Spirit'
(Eph. 5:18), in which he exhorts his hearers/readers: 'All who
duly appreciate the Spirit's operations and his thoughts of
peace toward them, and continue in meditation, longing,
desire, and prayer in the Spirit and for the Spirit, shall be
filled... They receive larger and larger measures from day to
day, and these are still further amplified in the course of every
trial encountered in the cause of Christ, and by every arduous
duty performed...'[19]

George Smeaton discerned that an emphasis on the Holy Spirit was at the heart of true experiential religion, and that it was experiential religion that gave vitality to the church. He knew this from his own spiritual experiences, dating back to the blessed years at the outset of his studies in Edinburgh when he mixed with M'Cheyne, the Bonars, and other spiritual men of that time who knew in their lives the operations of the Spirit of God. Sadly, he had seen this decline and give place to a formalism which left little place for the work of the Spirit of God in the soul. Respectability in the late nineteenth-century church lay in scholarship and literary preaching. This bred a nominality which became the blight of Scottish church life in the twentieth century. Yet it is precisely Smeaton's work which will continue to point to the source of real spiritual blessing in the church, through the necessity of the operations of the Holy Spirit in the life of a living, witnessing church.

14.
Other published writings

The pieces from Smeaton … show him to have possessed an acute theological mind as well as a wide acquaintance with the literature and discernment of theological error.

14.
Other published writings

An important area of special interest for Smeaton was in church/state relations, or the place and position of the civil magistrate in supporting the Christian religion, as we have seen from the Union controversy, discussed elsewhere.

In 1871, at the height of the Union controversy in the Free Church, Smeaton made two distinct contributions in that area. First of all there was his *National Christianity and Scriptural Union* (Edinburgh, 1871). John Macleod describes this book fulsomely as 'one of the fullest and most luminous expositions one can see of the historic Scottish Reformed view of church and State or of national religion'.[1] This was a substantial work of 124 pages.

In addition to this, in 1871 Smeaton also produced an edition of a standard work by Thomas M'Crie: 'Statement of difference between the profession of the Reformed Church of Scotland, as adopted by the seceders, and the profession contained in the new testimony and other acts lately adopted by the General Associate Synod: particularly on the power of the civil magistrate respecting religion, national reformation, etc.' This had been first produced in 1807 on the occasion of controversy within the Secession churches. Smeaton characterized it in this way: 'It is a masterly defence of the principle of Establishments as a Scripture truth; and the most complete vindication ever given to the world of the position occupied by the Reformed Church of Scotland on the whole subject of national religion, and of the magistrate's legitimate power in promoting it.'

Four years later Smeaton published *The Scottish Theory of Ecclesiastical Establishments* (Edinburgh, 1875), arising from a lecture given at the invitation of the Glasgow Conservative Association. This booklet is a mini-classic on the subject. More or less lost and forgotten, after a century this address is available from Still Waters Revival Books. This book is described as: 'a clear and concise summary of the biblical doctrine of the moral person (i.e. that God regards churches and nations as moral entities separate from the individual members of which they are composed). No Christian can afford not to understand this vital teaching!'[2]

On this subject, too, the influence of George Smeaton, reflected in the soundness and quality of his work, lives after him. Though Smeaton's perspective on the church and State issues seems for the greater part alien to modern Christian thought, his work on the subject nonetheless represents a challenge to the church, practically speaking, to think through the meaning and application of the headship of Christ over nations.

George Smeaton from time to time produced tracts and pamphlets, and some sermons and lectures were printed separately. He frequently contributed to the periodicals of the day, and he produced many contributions to *The British and Foreign Evangelical Review*, the outstanding theological journal of the day of which William Cunningham was editor from 1855 to 1860. Smeaton took over as editor after Cunningham, though he only served as such till 1863. Unfortunately, at that time articles were not attributed. Some of George Smeaton's contributions, however, have been identified, not least through his own references, especially in the appendix to his first volume on the atonement. (These are noted in the bibliography, section four: 'magazine articles'.)

It is to be assumed that there were many other articles from his pen, which have not been identified as his. The pieces from Smeaton that we can identify show him to have possessed an acute theological mind as well as a wide acquaintance with the literature and discernment of theological error.

Another feature of Smeaton's writings which should not be overlooked is the endorsements he gave to the writings of others. These give an interesting and significant insight into the range of his interests beyond the specific areas of his own published writings. Thus, his interest in revivals is reflected in his tract, *The Improvement of a Revival Time*, and an introductory paper to an edition of *The Beauties of the Rev. Ralph Erskine*, on the 'Suitableness of Erskine's writings to a period of religious revivals', both penned around 1860. In commenting on the suitableness of Ralph Erskine's writings for a period of revival, Smeaton says, 'These writings adapt themselves peculiarly to a revival period from their unction, amplitude and freshness, affording satisfaction in no ordinary way to the understanding and the heart.'[3]

His concerns with preaching and pastoral issues are reflected in his prefaces to the *Outlines of Discourses* of the late Rev. James Stewart (1860), and *Means and Methods to be Adopted for a Successful Ministry* by John Angell James (1861). His concern for a holy walk is reflected in his preface to Henry Darling's *The Closer Walk* (1862).[4] It is also reflected in the preface to a little-known volume, *Memorials of the Late Miss Agnes Aitken* (1882). The book comprised diary extracts and other recorded spiritual sayings of a pious lady who had been known to him. Speaking of the usefulness of these sayings and comments, Smeaton remarks on how they were fitted to call attention to the means of aspiring to great things in religion: 'The personal', he says, 'is often forgotten or absorbed in mere restless activity. But to expect great usefulness without great holiness is to expect the end without the means.'[5] This is a point as valid today as for any period of history.

We have already referred to his concern over changes in worship in relation to the matter of the introduction of instrumental music, highlighted in his preface to John M'Ewan's pamphlet on that subject (1883). Rather earlier, he wrote a preface to a volume on *The Lord's Day* by the continental writer Johannes Gossner (1860).[6] On this subject he did leave a notebook with extensive notes regarding the Lord's day and its proper observance. If he had a mind to produce a volume on that subject, that was never brought to fruition. This notebook is now lodged in the New College Library.

Then of course there were editions he produced, with introductions, of the work of Thomas Chalmers on the inspiration of the Old and New Testaments, and the statement of Thomas M'Crie on the matter of national Christianity, also referred to above. These latter were among his primary concerns in controversial areas in the course of his long ministry and professorial work. But all these prefaces and introductions do give an insight into the range of his concerns for the work and prosperity of the cause of the Lord Jesus Christ in his day.

It is often said of historic Calvinism that it is restrictive and 'narrow' and has been culturally stultifying. This of course is a caricature, because in Calvinism, says B. B. Warfield, 'Objectively speaking, theism comes to its rights; subjectively speaking, the religious relation attains its purity; soteriologically speaking, evangelical religion finds at length its full expression and its secure stability.'[7] It is no less than Christianity in its highest and most biblical expression. Its formative principles are the sovereignty of God and the particularity of grace. Far from being narrow, it embraces a coherent world-and-life view. We can concur with what William Hastie wrote about historic Calvinism in 1899: '[It] is the only system in which the whole order of the world is brought into a rational unity with the doctrine of grace... It is only with such a universal conception of God, established in a living way, that we can face, with hope of complete conquest, all the spiritual dangers and terrors of our time... But it is deep enough and large enough and divine enough, rightly understood, to confront them and do battle with them all in vindication of the Creator, Preserver, and Governor of the world, and of the justice and love of the divine Personality.'[8]

This is exactly how George Smeaton saw things. His view, as a fervent upholder of the doctrines of grace, was an expansive one. This is clear from his view of the application of the headship of Christ in relation to politics and the State, as we have seen. However, it is also clear from his very first lecture as professor of theology in the Free Church College at Aberdeen, delivered on Tuesday, 7 November 1854, in which he uttered these sublime words:

Is there a department of human action from which the glorifying influences of the divine life is to be inter-cepted, and on which the doleful inscription is to be read, 'Here Christ does not dwell'? On the contrary, Christianity is destined to glorify everything; in all art, all science, all literature, all scenes and relations of hu-man life, should only be vessels to contain the heavenly treasure. All the spheres of action are to be regarded as the outward scenes in which the manifestation of the divine life, flowing from Jesus of Nazareth, is to develop itself. And nothing, along the whole flight of time, is to be withdrawn from the sanctifying and ennobling power of that divine life which is hid in him, the life-source of ages. There is nothing to be drawn between the human mind and the personal Redeemer, either to obscure the beams of his light, or to intercept the communications of his life. And it is the part of theology on the one side, and of the activities of the church on the other, to unite their efforts to remove every intervening obstacle, until all shall be irradiated by his life, and holiness to the Lord shall be written upon all.[9]

This was a perspective to which George Smeaton consis-tently held throughout his ministry and teaching work, and it surely speaks with power every bit as much to the church in the twenty-first century as it did to his own day.

15.
Eventide

'He [George Smeaton]
pointed many souls to
heaven, and he has led the
way. And while we thank
God for his life and
labours, may the
remembrance of them
quicken us to follow in his
footsteps, even as he
followed Christ's.'

15.
Eventide

In their time in Edinburgh, George and Janet Smeaton had the sadness of losing their eldest two children. Their daughter Isabella died on 12 August 1862, aged nineteen. On her gravestone in the Grange Cemetery they had inscribed, 'for ever with the Lord'. Their oldest son George went in to the Bengal Civil Service. He went out to India in October 1864 and 'graduated' in that service in 1869. From August 1869 he was an assistant manager and (tax) collector in Shahabad, a district of British India in the Patna division of Bengal. Sadly, he died in Southampton on his way back from India on 19 December 1870. He was twenty-nine years old and unmarried. His parents put under his name on the gravestone in the Grange Cemetery, 'Thy will be done', an inscription not as assured as the one inscribed for Isabella.

For someone of the conservative sympathies of George Smeaton, his later years must have exercised his righteous soul. He was after all like-minded with his friend James Begg (1808-83). He was closely associated with Newington Free Church, of which Begg was minister for forty years until his death. Smeaton often filled the pulpit in the minister's absence. It was his sad duty to conduct one of the funeral sermons, on 7 October 1883, after Begg's death. The other funeral sermon was preached by John Kennedy of Dingwall (1819-84), who himself was with the Lord within seven months. The loss of such like-minded colleagues affected Smeaton deeply as he witnessed the emergence of a very different Free Church from the one he had known in earlier days. Smeaton himself, clearly out of concern for innovations in the Grange, after 1884 moved to Buccleuch Free Church, where the minister was

Robert Gordon (1823-1909). Subsequently Gordon and most of the congregation did not go into the union of the Free and United Presbyterian Churches in 1900. Gordon's father of the same name had been one of the most prominent of the Free Church ministers in Disruption days.

George Smeaton, 1882

In February 1889 the second edition of Smeaton's work on the Holy Spirit came out. Suddenly, on Sabbath, 14 April that year, just after the close of session in New College, and having reached his jubilee in the ministry the previous month, he peacefully passed into the presence of his Lord.

His friend and colleague at New College, Thomas Smith, described the circumstances: 'After spending the last day of his life in the discharge of important professorial duty, writing kindly letters to a student, to a former student and friend, and to his colleague, Dr Duns,[1] enjoying the converse of the beloved one who had shared his joys and sorrows for well nigh half a century, after sleeping apparently through the night the sleep which God gives to his beloved, on Sabbath morning he uttered a great shriek of momentary bodily pain, and ere it had ceased to pierce the ear of her who heard it, the earthly note of anguish was transmuted into the strain of the heavenly Hallelujah!' Medically speaking he died from *angina pectoris.* Smith movingly ends his funeral oration with these words: 'In contemplation of such a scene each one of us may well say, "Let me die the death of the righteous, and let my last end be like his!"'[2]

For his part, Robert Gordon concludes his appreciation of Smeaton with these moving words: 'He pointed many souls to heaven, and he has led the way. And while we thank God for his life and labours, may the remembrance of them quicken us to follow in his footsteps, even as he followed Christ's.'[3] These funeral sermons were preached by Robert Gordon and Thomas Smith in Buccleuch Free Church, West Crosscauseway, on Sabbath, 21 April 1889. His last earthly remains had been laid to rest in the Grange Cemetery a few days earlier. Janet Smeaton survived her husband by just four years. She died 1 March 1893 and was buried with her husband in the family plot in the Grange.

The Smeatons' youngest son, who became popularly known as Oliphant Smeaton, returned home to Britain after his mother's death in 1893. He had been educated in Edin-burgh (Royal High School and University) and seemed destined for the ministry. Apparently, however, he had difficulty subscribing to the *Confession of Faith* and he did not follow through preparations for the ministry in Scotland. In 1878 he emigrated to New Zealand in his twenty-second year, initially with a view to work with the Presbyterian church there. He completed one year of theological study under the Auckland Presbytery and was engaged for a six-month period as a home mission evangelist in Helensville, Auckland, but he did not continue in that work. Instead he successfully pursued a career first in teaching and then in journalism and other literary interests, including novel writing.

While in New Zealand, Oliphant married Wilhelmine Clark in 1882. Oliphant and Wilhelmine had one daughter, Aileen,

in 1883. The family moved to Australia that year, initially
being based in Melbourne, before they returned to Scotland
after the death of Oliphant's mother in 1893. They maintained the family home at 13 Mansionhouse Road (later
number 37) and associated with the congregation of Grange
Free Church (Grange United Free Church, after 1900).
During the ministry of the Rev. William Ewing, editor of the
Annals of the Free Church of Scotland, 1843-1900 (with
which Oliphant Smeaton provided assistance), the younger
Smeaton became an elder in 1909.

The history of that congregation records that, 'He was the
last survivor of the company who first met in his father's
dining room for worship before the church was formed. As a
boy he had played with his companions among the piles of
materials gathered for the building of the church. He had a
great love for the church all his days. He lived abroad for some
years, and when he returned he renewed his association with
the Grange. Appointed Session Clerk, he was involved in all
its interests and activities.'[4]

Oliphant Smeaton became a well-known figure in the literary circles of the day and is perhaps best known as editor of
the *Famous Scots* series produced around the turn of the
century. He died on 31 March 1914 and was survived by his
wife Wilhelmine (1859-1931) and their daughter. He was
buried in the family plot in the Grange Cemetery, where his
wife was also later buried.[5]

Oliphant and Wilhelmine's daughter, Elizabeth Aileen
Hamilton Smeaton, was born in Whangarei, some 100 miles
north of Auckland in the North Island of New Zealand, in
1883. She was George and Janet Smeaton's only grandchild.
Five years old when her grandfather died in 1889, she was to
say that she had heard of her grandfather that, 'He seemed to
live so much in heaven that he did not have much contact
with earth.'[6]

Gravestone of George Smeaton, Grange Cemetery, Edinburgh

Aileen Smeaton returned with her parents to Scotland after her grandmother's death in 1893. Subsequently she married one John Davidson, a United Free Church of Scotland minister,[7] with whom she had seven children. The oldest, Wilma, became a missionary in India and married William Stewart, a Scottish preacher in the United Church of India. Then there was John, who became a Church of Scotland minister in Sanquhar.[8] Oliphant became a paper-maker; Anna a 'church sister'; George an eye doctor in Durban in South Africa; Allan, a history teacher; and finally Aileen, who became a nurse. Aileen (the mother) lived latterly in Edinburgh, where she passed away on 31 July 1952, aged sixty-eight. Her husband had died on 22 November 1945. There is an inscription for her on the lower left hand side of the Smeaton headstone in the Grange Cemetery.

16.
A learned and pious man

George Smeaton was an outstanding scholar. The quality of his teaching and his grasp of literature and Bible truth is clear from his books...

16.
A learned and pious man

In an inaugural lecture given in New College in 1889, Marcus Dods, who succeeded George Smeaton in the Chair of exegetical theology and who was a man of very different outlook, was to acknowledge this of his predecessor: 'Not only had he the ordinary acquirements of a teacher of exegesis, exact scholarship and acquaintance with modern criticism, but he had a quite exceptional theological learning.' Dods goes on to say, 'I do not know if any man is left among us who is so much at home as he was in Patristic and mediaeval writers.'[1]

Smeaton's colleague and friend Thomas Smith was of the same opinion as Dods: 'I do not know that in this country there is, or ever has been, a man more accurately conversant with all the great theological schools, the Patristic, the Mediaeval, the Reformation, the Puritan, the Dutch and the modern German. It was said to me the other day by one well qualified to judge, that the erudition of the late Dr Cunningham might be more minute in regards to the third of these schools, but was far inferior to Dr Smeaton's with regard to the others.'[2]

It is quite clear that George Smeaton was an outstanding scholar. The quality of his teaching and his grasp of literature and Bible truth is clear from his books, the continuing value of which ensures their durability as statements of the Reformed and evangelical faith. It is interesting to note that in a preface to a 1996 edition of Patrick Fairbairn's Cunningham Lectures on *The Revelation of Law in Scripture* (1869), Sinclair B. Ferguson wrote of Fairbairn that 'With Smeaton,

he must be reckoned one of the outstanding biblical theologians of the nineteenth century.'

Apparently, when he died Dr Smeaton left a personal
library of some 15,000 books, including some volumes from
Reformation and pre-Reformation periods! Most of these
were donated to New College Library, Edinburgh. Oliphant
Smeaton wrote that at the time of his death, his father's
library 'numbered considerably over 15,000 volumes, and
was as varied as it was choice. I had the privilege of presenting it, afterwards, to the New College, where now it remains.'[3]

In assessing George Smeaton's work as a theologian and
exegete, a familiarity with his writings inevitably impresses
one with his phenomenal grasp of his subject. His work is
painstaking, and it is clear that he has a very thorough
acquaintance with the literature and discussions of the day.
In all his work there is clear evidence of a profound acceptance of the authority of holy Scripture as the inspired and
inerrant Word of God and utterly trustworthy record of
divine revelation. One can readily agree with John
Macleod's assessment that, 'A man can take his word in
regard to any theme that he handles as soon as that of any
writer on theological subjects.'[4]

Smeaton's commitment to the whole doctrine of the Westminster Confession of Faith is evident. Yet his concern was
not just to argue back from dogmatics, but to establish the
truth on exegetical grounds.[5] Sadly, with the changes in views
of the inspiration and authority of the Scriptures, and with the
consequent change in theological fashion, Smeaton's work,
for all its exceptional cogency and quality, was not given the
place it merited in his own day. Nevertheless, acquaintance
with his writings, and not least the contributions he made to
The British and Foreign Evangelical Review which are attrib-
utable to him, may well persuade one that James MacGregor
was not far from the mark when he said of Smeaton that he
had 'the best constituted theological intellect in Christen-

dom'.[6] MacGregor, a colleague of Smeaton at New College between 1868 and 1881, was no mean judge. In their book *The Free Church of Scotland: The Crisis of 1900*, Alexander Stewart and J. Kennedy Cameron stated fairly of George Smeaton that he 'was perhaps the most learned theologian in the Free Church, and a man of deep and unaffected godliness'.[7]

Apart from his theological learning, George Smeaton was highly regarded for his piety. The Kirk Session of Newington Free Church recorded this tribute after his passing: He was a man, they said, 'of singular benevolence and sweetness of disposition, universally beloved for his goodness, as well as highly esteemed for his work's sake, and respected for his moral worth and the constancy of his life and character. He was eminently distinguished for genuine piety, and for following after peace with all men, and personal holiness... As a pastor and preacher of the gospel he was highly appreciated, especially by the most spiritually minded of his hearers, for the earnest simplicity and solemnity of his manner, the force of his teaching, the clearness of his views, the vigour and valour of his defence of the truth and the richness of his Christian experience.'[8]

He was 'a man of God', said a tribute from the Free Church Defence Association, of which he was a valued member, 'and one who had much sweet communion with Jesus. He had a deeply spiritual mind. He seemed to look upon all things in the light of eternity, in the relation they bore to the glory of God and the good of immortal souls.' This tribute adds, tellingly: 'The Constitutional Party in the Free Church has lost one of its chief supports, and that loss is more especially felt at this time when so many faithful ministers and laymen have so recently been removed from our midst.'[9]

On 4 June 1889, the General Assembly of the Free Church adopted the following appreciation of Professor Smeaton:

> By the death of Professor Smeaton, which took place on 14 April, the church has lost one whose many gifts and great graces were for an ornament and for strength to her. A man of massive intellect and unwearied diligence, of profound erudition and exact scholarship, he consecrated his talents, his time and the wealth of his learning to the service of God, and the interpretation of his holy Word. As an occupant of the Chair he held, first in Aberdeen and then in Edinburgh, he loved his work; for with his whole heart he loved the Word of God, which was his only textbook. To him it was a most congenial task, while he expounded and applied the canons of biblical criticism, to discourse to his students of the great verities of New Testament Scripture, and the great themes of evangelical preaching — grace, propitiation, regeneration, righteousness and eternal life. In his dealings with the students, he commended himself to every man's conscience. As himself an ardent and reverent student of the Word, and an humble and prayerful saint, the influence he exercised over very many of those who are now, or have been, able ministers of the Free Church, has been seen and felt in the character of their ministry and their manner of handling the Word of God. Dr Smeaton's works on the teaching of the Master and his apostles, on the nature and scope of the atonement, are valuable contributions to the literature of the subject; and in connection with his tenure of the Cunningham Lectureship, he chose a fitting theme for his sanctified learning, when he set forth the doctrine of the Holy Ghost.
>
> Dr Smeaton was a man of singular sweet, sympathetic and guileless nature — a man greatly beloved for

his goodness, and respected for his thorough consistency and blameless integrity. Above all, he was distinguished for his genuine piety and purity of heart, and for following after peace with all men, and personal holiness. As a pastor and preacher of the gospel he was highly esteemed, especially by the most spiritually minded of our people, for his earnest simplicity and solemn gladness, his felicitous way of comparing Scripture with Scripture, for the force and faithfulness of his warning and teaching, the clearness of his spiritual discernment, the soundness and justice of his views, the vigour and valour of his defence of the truth and the richness of his Christian experience.

Dr Smeaton was a man absolutely without an enemy. He took little part in the business of church courts, and but seldom descended into the arena of controversy; yet he held decided opinions and gave no uncertain sound on the debated questions which from time to time arise in the church, and his godly sincerity, his loyalty to truth, and his moderation, were known unto all men.

The General Assembly render thanks to the great Head of the church for raising up such a man as Professor Smeaton, and sparing him so long, permitting him to complete full fifty years of ordained ministerial and professorial service. Dr Smeaton was very suddenly called away from his labours, but even while men were startled and grieved by the unexpected tidings of his death, they felt that it was meet that such an one as he should be swiftly translated, for his conversation was in heaven, and his affections were set upon things above: 'He walked with God; and he was not; for God took him.'[10]

In his obituary notice of Professor Smeaton in *The Free Church of Scotland Monthly* of 2 September 1889, J. G. Cunningham summed up Smeaton's life as a minister of Christ in terms of the verse, 'We will give ourselves to prayer,

and to the ministry of the Word' (Acts 6:4). Said Cunningham: 'The direct, earnest, and varied requests which flowed
from his lips in public prayer were manifestly the utterances of
one who was accustomed to be much alone with God.'[11]

'All who had the privilege of friendship with him,' said
Robert Gordon in his memorial sermon, 'his daily walk and
conversation made clearly manifest the strength of the bond
that united him to God. His genuine humility of spirit, his
steadfast hold of divine truth, his fearless defence of everything which concerned the honour and glory of God — all
these warranted men, as they thought of or looked upon him
to say — "Thou man of God".'[12]

Smeaton's portrait was painted by Robert Gibb, ARSA
(1845-1932), late in the subject's life. Throughout the last few
decades of the nineteenth century, Gibb painted several
portraits of important Scotsmen, particularly clerics and
academics. (Gibbs' reputation, however, was built on his
military paintings. Perhaps his greatest work was a painting
entitled *The Thin Red Line*, which appeared in 1881. This
was apparently inspired by Alexander Kinglake's account of
the 93rd Highlanders at Balaclava in his book *The Invasion of
the Crimea*.) The Smeaton portrait was gifted by Mrs Smeaton to New College in 1892. It was hung in the Common
Hall, to look down on generations of students who, sadly,
would take a very different line from Smeaton himself in the
understanding of the faith. Unfortunately the portrait is no
longer in the possession of New College. In the 1990s it was
auctioned off by Phillips in Edinburgh (now Bonhams) and
fell into the possession of an American antiquarian bookseller
from Pennsylvania. It fetched less than £500.

George Smeaton stands as a monument to the very best of
Scottish theology, and through the reprinting of his greatest
works of theology and biblical exposition 'He being dead yet
speaketh' (Heb. 11:4). The church is still blessed and edified
by these products of his devout and fruitful life. To the end it
is clear that George Smeaton's greatest concern was for the

souls of men; that they should hear the Word of God clearly and make response to Christ, to whom all men everywhere are invited to believe and to yield obedience. He was throughout his life driven by the reality that all must appear before the great white throne to give an account.

For ministers, that will be an awesome day. And an awesome day it will be for all people, not least those who have sat under clear and faithful gospel preaching calling them to repent and believe: 'What an awakening thought it must be to not a few that every sermon and every expostulation must be brought back to mind! You have to meet again, and to give in the mutual account; and every entreaty to accept Christ and flee from the wrath to come will be flashed back upon your memory in the light of the judge's countenance. There will be no forgotten sermons on that day: they can be recalled from the tablets of memory, and they will be so recalled. O, let the recollection of them move you now to accept the great salvation!'[13]

In similar vein George Smeaton closed his sermon on the death of his friend James Begg. This gives a clear indication of his passion for souls, even in his seventieth year, and is an appropriate note on which to conclude this sketch of the life of a faithful man of God:

One parting word to you all: Follow him as he followed Christ, and only as he followed Christ. 'Whose faith follow', says the apostle. The converted in the congregation, whom he regarded as his joy and crown of rejoicing, will meet him in the presence of the Lord at his coming. The unconverted in the congregation, and in this city and land, who often heard that manly and bold confessor of the truth, have a great responsibility. How will you be able, in the great day of the Lord, to meet him in the presence of that Lord and Saviour to whom you were so urgently and tenderly invited, from day to day? O, remember how times and opportunities pass away.

Photo of the Robert Gibb painting of George Smeaton
(owned by D. C. Lachman)

That voice you will hear no more. And yet you have not done with those sermons, invitations and appeals, which followed one another during that precious and long-protracted ministry. They will all be recalled in eternity to your woe and agony, if they fail, in your recollection of them, to influence you and move you to accept the great salvation. O, may the Spirit of illumination yet descend on you, to melt you and subdue you. How often has he said, 'Come. Come, for all things are ready! We beseech you, in Christ's stead, be ye reconciled to God.'[14]

Endnotes

Preface

1. George Smeaton, *Memoir of Alexander Thomson of Banchory* (Edinburgh, 1869), p.1.
2. George Smeaton, *The Doctrine of the Atonement as Taught by Christ Himself* (1868, first ed.; 1871, second ed.); *The Doctrine of the Atonement as Taught by the Apostles* (1870).
3. George Smeaton, *The Doctrine of the Holy Spirit* (1882, first ed.; 1889, second ed.).
4. John Macleod, *Scottish Theology,* (Edinburgh, 1946, second ed.), p.289. John Macleod (1872-1948) was a professor in various Chairs in the Free Church College, Edinburgh, after 1906 up to his retirement in 1942. He was Principal of the college between 1927 and 1942. This was the theological college of the continuing Free Church after 1900 and should not be confused with New College, which at that date became the college of the United Free Church. The United Free Church came about as a result of a union of the majority of the Free Church and the United Presbyterian Church of Scotland in 1900. Reference is made to this elsewhere.
5. See the bibliography, special studies section.
6. Macleod, *Scottish Theology*, p.288. Macleod refers here to William Cunningham (1805-61), professor of church history (1845-61) and Principal (1847-61) at New College, Edinburgh, the theological hall of the Free Church of Scotland which had emerged after the 'Disruption' from the Church of Scotland in 1843. Cunningham's major books on *Historical Theology* (two volumes, 1862) and *The Reformers and the Theology of the Reformation* (1862) have been reprinted by the Banner of Truth Trust in recent years.
7. Macleod, *Scottish Theology*, p.289. As with many of the details in Macleod's excellent work, the source of this anecdote is not given. James MacGregor (1830-94), a native of Callander, Perthshire, was professor of systematic theology in New College, Edinburgh, between 1868 and 1881. He emigrated to New Zealand in 1881 and became minister of Columba Church, Oamaru (1882-94), in the Synod of Otago and Southland. MacGregor was a conservative theologian though erratic at some points, such as his strange support for William Robertson Smith, though he had no sympathy with the higher critics!
8. See the bibliography, books and pamphlets section.

9. H. L. Goddard, 'The contribution of George Smeaton (1814-89) to theological thought', PhD thesis (University of Edinburgh, 1953). Goddard's thesis is dated 1953, although the PhD was not awarded until 1960.

10. N. P. Madsen, 'Atonement and pneumatology: a study in the theology of George Smeaton', PhD thesis (University of St Andrew's, 1974), p.73.

11. Madsen, 'Atonement and pneumatology', p.32.

12. Smeaton, *The Doctrine of the Atonement as Taught by Christ Himself* (Edinburgh, 1871, second ed.), p.439.

13. R. M. Shillaker, 'The federal pneumatology of George Smeaton (1814-89)', PhD thesis (Highland Theological College, 2002), p.1. 'Federal' is from the Latin *foedus*, meaning 'covenant'. 'Pneumatology' is from a Greek word *pneuma* which means (among other things) 'Spirit', and thus *pneumatology* refers to the doctrine and work of the Holy Spirit.

14. Shillaker, 'Federal pneumatology', p.2.

15. In a Presbyterian church such as the Church of Scotland or Free Church of Scotland, the General Assembly is the supreme ruling body. It meets once a year and comprises representatives of ministers and elders from throughout the church. Normally one minister in three or four would attend in any year, with one elder appointed for each minister. The church is made up of presbyteries corresponding to congregations within given geographical areas by which the country is divided up for practical purposes. The presbyteries would appoint the ministers and elders to the General Assemblies. Presbyteries oversee the work of the congregations within their area and are made up of ministers and elders (one for each congregation) from each of these local congregations.

16. *The Scotsman*, 15 April 1889, p.7.

17. Goddard, pp.181-2.

18. M. A. Kinnear, 'Scottish New Testament scholarship and the atonement, c.1845-1920', PhD thesis (University of Edinburgh, 1995), p.179. The third chapter of this thesis deals specifically with 'George Smeaton and the development of the Calvinist view of the atonement' (pp.124-79).

19. Smeaton, *The Doctrine of the Atonement as Taught by Christ Himself* (1871, second ed.), pp.415-96.

20. William Knight, *Some Nineteenth-Century Scotsmen* (Edinburgh and London, 1903), pp.108-15.

Chapter 1

1. Hew Scott, *Fasti Ecclesiae Scoticanae*, (Edinburgh, 1925), vol. 5. George Smeaton is described as 'grand-nephew of John S., the engineer' (p.154). In an entry in *Who Was Who, 1897-1916*, for George Smeaton's son, Oliphant, it is stated that Oliphant Smeaton was the

great-grand-nephew of John Smeaton. However, the more recent volume *John Smeaton, FRS* (London, 1981), edited by Professor A. W. Skempton, says that John Smeaton had only one brother who died aged four (p.7). Unless there is a mistake there, it may be that rather than grand-uncle of George Smeaton, John Smeaton was a cousin of George Smeaton's grandfather.

2. For details of John Smeaton see *Dictionary of National Biography*, Volume XVIII, 1921-22, reprinted by Oxford University Press, p.393.

3. Oliphant Smeaton, 'Professor Smeaton and his colleagues', in William Knight, *Some Nineteenth-Century Scotsmen* (Edinburgh, 1903), p.108.

4. Translation: 'He [Thomas Smeton] being well acquainted with the practises of the papists, namely, Jesuits, and their devices for subverting the Kirk of Scotland, both publicly and privately, ceased not to cry and warn ministers and scholars to be diligent upon their charges and books, to study the controversies, and to take heed they neglected not the time, and there would be a strong unseat[ing] of papists. Also, he was careful to know the religion and affection of noble men, insinuating him[self] into that company, in a wise and grave manner, and warning them to beware of evil company, and not to send their bairns [children] to dangerous parties [teachers, influences]. And, finally, Mr Andrew [Melville] and he [Thomas Smeton] marvellously conspiring in purposes and judgements, were the first motioners [movers], of an anti-seminary to be erected in St Andrew's to the Jesuit seminaries, for the course of theology, and never ceased at Assemblies and court, till that work was begun and set forward.'

5. For details of Thomas Smeton, see Wodrow's 'Life of Smeton', apud MSS. in Bibl. Acad. Glasg., vol i. See also James Melville's *Diary*, pp.56-58; and Thomas M'Crie's *Life of Andrew Melville*, second edition (Edinburgh, 1824), vol. i., pp.158-62; vol. ii, pp.379-83. See also Hew Scott, DD, *Fasti Ecclesiae Scoticanae*, vol. III — Synod of Glasgow and Ayr (Edinburgh, 1920), p.410.

6. Thomas apparently died in 1657. This detail is recorded in Scott, *Fasti Ecclesiae Scoticanae*, vol. III, p.410. In his *Life of Andrew Melville* (1824, second ed.), Thomas M'Crie says that 'Thomas Smeton, made AM at Glasgow in 1604, was probably his son' (vol. I, p.194, footnote).

7. Scott, *Fasti Ecclesiae Scoticanae*, vol. III, p.410.

8. M'Crie, vol. II, p.383.

Chapter 2

1. *In Memoriam: Sermons Preached in Buccleuch Free Church, Sabbath, 21 April 1889, on the Death of the Rev. George Smeaton, DD* (Edinburgh, 1889), p.35. Thomas Smith (1817-1906) was professor of evan-

gelistic theology (missions) at New College (1880-92). The biographer
of James Begg, he was of the same conservative outlook as Smeaton on
all the controversial issues that arose in the Free Church in those days.
2. *In Memoriam*, p.35.
3. As above.
4. *In Memoriam*, p.37.
5. William Knight, *Some Nineteenth-Century Scotsmen* (Edinburgh and
   London, 1903), p.109.
6. William Arnot, *Memoir of the Late James Halley, AB* (Edinburgh, 1842,
   second ed.), p.86. Halley died tragically young, in 1841, aged twenty-
   seven.
7. *In Memoriam*, pp.36-37.
8. John Macleod, *Scottish Theology* (Edinburgh, 1946, second ed.),
   p.287.
9. For ten years up to 1843, controversy raged in the Church of Scotland
   over the powers of patrons — usually the wealthy landlords or landed
   gentry — to appoint ministers to parish church congregations in their
   area. This was allowed by the Patronage Act of 1712. The ten years'
   conflict was over the issue of the spiritual independence of the church
   from state interference in its affairs. The 'conflict' polarized the church
   between the growing numbers of evangelicals and the so-called 'mod-
   erates' who had held sway in the Kirk up to the early 1830s. It was the
   evangelicals, by and large, who opposed the Patronage Act. This conflict resulted in a significant number of ministers and people leaving the
   Church of Scotland to form the Free Church of Scotland in May 1843.
   That event was known as the 'Disruption'. More direct reference is
   made to this elsewhere in this book.
10. A. A. Bonar, *Memoir and Remains of the Rev. Robert Murray
    M'Cheyne* (Edinburgh, 1844), p.40. In the enlarged edition of the
    Memoir issued in 1892, the reference to the Exegetical Society is found
    on pages 29 and 30. An additional appendix is found on pages 177
    and following of that edition, in which Bonar provides some biographi-
    cal detail of his friends. His reference to George Smeaton is found on
    page 184. It is this 1892 edition that was reprinted by the Banner of
    Truth Trust for the first time in 1966.
11. James Buchanan (1804-70) went into the Free Church at the Disrup-
    tion of 1843. He became professor first in the apologetics chair at New
    College (1845-48) before transferring to the chair of systematic theology
    (1848-68). He is particularly remembered for his book, *The Office and
    Work of the Holy Spirit* (1842) and his Cunningham Lectures on *The
    Doctrine of Justification* (1867), both of which have been reprinted in
    recent years by the Banner of Truth Trust. He was minister in North
    Leith from 1828 to 1840.

Chapter 3

1. Bond in the Scottish Records Office: CH2/486/58. The value of money has changed immeasurably since the early part of the nineteenth century. In broad terms, a multiplier of 150-200 times might be applied to provide some idea of a modern-day equivalent amount. It is said that the average Victorian family subsisted on less than £1 a week.
2. J. G. Cunningham, *The Free Church of Scotland Monthly*, 2 September 1889, p.279.
3. Martyrs Memorial Reformed Presbyterian Church became Martyrs Free Church at the union of the Free and Reformed Presbyterian Churches in 1876. Goold continued to be the active minister in the Martyrs Free Church up till 1896. Apparently Smeaton occupied Goold's pulpit at Martyrs the Sabbath before his death, 7 April 1889. It should be noted that in 1863 the Reformed Presbyterian Church of Scotland had divided into majority and minority synods. It was the majority synod that entered the Free Church in 1876. The minority synod continued as the Reformed Presbyterian Church of Scotland. Only three small congregations remain, in Airdrie, Stranraer and Wishaw.
4. *In Memoriam: Sermons Preached in Buccleuch Free Church, Sabbath, 21 April 1889, on the Death of the Rev. George Smeaton, DD* (Edinburgh, 1889), p.39. In his obituary notice of George Smeaton in *The Free Church of Scotland Monthly*, 2 September 1889, the Rev. J. G. Cunningham states that there were two daughters who died young.
5. *In Memoriam*, pp.37-38.
6. The sermon first appeared in the *Free Church Pulpit* (Perth: James Dewar and Son, 1845), vol. I, pp.587-97. It was reproduced in the *Banner of Truth* magazine, August 1959. See *The Banner of Truth: Magazine Issues 1-16* (Edinburgh, 2005), pp.501-11.
7. In the Presbyterian church, a synod comprises a certain number of presbyteries appointed to meet together, for the government of the church. Synods cover a wider geographical area than presbyteries and have a responsibility for reviewing the work of presbyteries within their bounds. All members of all the related presbyteries will be members of the synod. Synods normally meet once a year.
8. George Smeaton, 'A witnessing church — a church baptized with the Holy Ghost' (Perth, 1846), p.7. This sermon was reproduced in the third volume of the *Free Church Pulpit* in 1847.
9. As above.
10. Smeaton, 'A witnessing church', p.9.
11. Smeaton, 'A witnessing church', pp.9-10.
12. Smeaton, 'A witnessing church', p.10.
13. Smeaton, 'A witnessing church', p.6.

14. Smeaton, 'A witnessing church', p.12. The reference here is to Thomas Hooker (1586-1647), the Puritan who fled from England to Holland in 1630 and from thence to America where in 1636 he helped found the colony at Hartford, Connecticut.
15. Smeaton, 'A witnessing church', p.13.
16. George Smeaton, 'The true preacher', in *The Christian Treasury* (Edinburgh, 1872), p.254.
17. Smeaton, 'The true preacher', p.256.
18. As above.
19. As above.
20. As above.
21. Smeaton, 'The true preacher', p.257.
22. Smeaton, 'The true preacher', p.257. See note 14.
23. George Smeaton, *The Improvement of a Revival Time* (Edinburgh, c.1860), pp.14-15. Uppercase and italics in the original.
24. George Smeaton, Introductory notice II, 'Suitableness of Erskine's writings to a period of religious revivals', in *The Beauties of the Rev. Ralph Erskine*, Samuel McMillan, ed. (Aberdeen, Edinburgh, London and Glasgow: A. Fullerton and Co., n.d. [1860]), pp.xxxvii-xxxviii.
25. George Smeaton, 'A faithful minister of Christ' [on Col. 1:7] in 'Sermons preached in Free St Matthew's Church, Bath Street, Glasgow, with special reference to the death of the Rev. Samuel Miller, DD', (Glasgow: John N. Mackinlay, 1881), p.13.
26. Smeaton, 'A faithful minister of Christ', pp.14-15.
27. Smeaton, 'A faithful minister of Christ', p.17.
28. George Smeaton, 'The confessing of Christ before men, and the promised reward' [on Matt. 10:32] in 'Sermons preached in Newington Free Church, Edinburgh, on the occasion of the death of the Rev. James Begg DD ... on Sabbath, 7 October 1883' (Edinburgh, 1883), p.22. Emphasis in printed sermon.
29. Smeaton, 'The confessing of Christ before men', p.26.

Chapter 4

1. The 'non-intrusionists' were those in the church who opposed the 'intrusion' of ministers into parishes by the local patrons, usually landed gentry, over the wishes of the members of the congregation.
2. Quoted in N. L. Walker, *Chapters from the History of the Free Church of Scotland* (Edinburgh, 1895), p.20.
3. A list of all the Disruption ministers and missionaries is found in Appendix I of Thomas Brown, *Annals of the Disruption* (Edinburgh, 1893), pp.797-813.

4. George Smeaton, *Memoir of Alexander Thomson of Banchory* (Edinburgh, 1869), p.289. Emphasis is Smeaton's.
5. Smeaton, *Memoir of Alexander Thomson*, p.290.
6. Smeaton, *Memoir of Alexander Thomson*, pp.290-1.
7. *Minutes*, Auchterarder Free Church, 5 August 1843.
8. *Minutes*, Cupar Free Church Presbytery, at Cupar on 22 August 1843.
9. H. L. Goddard, 'The contribution of George Smeaton (1814-89) to theological thought', PhD thesis (University of Edinburgh, 1953), pp.5-6.
10. J. G. Cunningham, *The Free Church of Scotland Monthly*, 2 September 1889, p. 279.
11. Rev. John M'Ewan in a funeral sermon in Newington Free Church, Edinburgh, on Sabbath, 21 April 1889, as reported in *The British Weekly*, Friday, 26 April 1889, p.421.

Chapter 5

1. William Knight, *Some Nineteenth-Century Scotsmen* (Edinburgh and London, 1903), p.110.
2. Patrick Fairbairn, interestingly, was also born in the Greenlaw area. He was ordained at North Ronaldsay (Orkney) in 1830. At the time of the Disruption (1843) when he entered the Free Church, he was minister at Saltoun in Midlothian. He was tutor, then professor at Aberdeen until 1856 when he was transferred to the Glasgow Free Church College, becoming principal the following year. Fairbairn is best known for his work on *The Typology of Scripture* (1845), a commentary of Ezekiel (1852), a work on *The Interpretation of Prophecy* (1856), his Cunningham Lectures on *The Revelation of Law in Scripture* (1868), and his editorship of *The Imperial Bible Dictionary* (1866). He was a faithful and conservative Bible scholar and theologian.
3. George Smeaton, 'The necessary harmony between doctrine and spiritual life' (Aberdeen, 1853), p.16. Emphasis is Smeaton's.
4. As above.
5. Smeaton, 'The necessary harmony', p.22.
6. Smeaton, 'The necessary harmony', pp.27-28.
7. PDGAFCS, 25 May 1854, p.137. The minutes in those days were very full and included annotations of approval or disapproval!
8. George Smeaton, 'The basis of Christian doctrine in divine fact' (Aberdeen, 1854), pp.3-4. Smeaton is here referring to David Brainerd (1718-47), Presbyterian missionary to native American tribes in North America; Felix Neff (1798-1829), a Swiss Protestant divine and philanthropist who devoted himself to evangelistic work in the valley of Freissinires, where he was so successful that he changed the character of the district and its inhabitants; and Robert Murray M'Cheyne (1813-43), a

powerful and godly Scottish preacher in the years before the Disruption (1843). These men all died young, but were greatly used of the Lord in their brief ministries.

9. W. Ewing, ed., *Annals of the Free Church of Scotland, 1843-1900* (Edinburgh, 1914), vol. I, p.133. Smeaton was to preach a funeral sermon after the death of Davidson, on 'The faithful labourer's reward in heaven' (from Dan. 12:3), in Aberdeen on Sabbath, 5 May 1872.

10. Ewing, *Annals of the Free Church*, p.49.

11. Knight, *Some Nineteenth-Century Scotsmen*, p.111.

Chapter 6

1. William Cousin (1812-83) was a staunch constitutionalist in later debates within the Free Church. He was later minister at Melrose (1859-78). His wife, Anne Ross Cousin (1824-1906) is well known as the composer of 'The sands of time are sinking', based on the last words of Samuel Rutherford.

2. PDGAFCS, 26 May 1857, pp.88-89. Edmonston's name is spelt 'Edmonstone' in W. Ewing, ed., *Annals of the Free Church of Scotland 1843-1900* (Edinburgh, 1914), vol. I, p.146. Ewing also has his year of death as 1895, which is certainly a misprint for 1865. Thomas Brown in his *Annals of the Disruption 1843* (Edinburgh, 1893), gives Edmonston's death as 8 December 1865 (see p.799).

3. PDGAFCS, 26 May 1857, p.90.

4. PDGAFCS, 28 May 1857, p.147.

5. William Knight, *Some Nineteenth-Century Scotsmen* (Edinburgh and London, 1903), pp.113-14. This comprises an extract from a letter of Smeaton's written ten years after Cunningham's death.

6. Each of the Free Church Colleges — in Edinburgh, Aberdeen and Glasgow — was visited every five years (thus 'quinquennial') by a committee of the General Assembly. The purpose was to ensure that they were functioning as they should in the interests of the preparation of men for the ministry of the church.

7. PDGAFCS, May 1858, Report of the special commission for the quinquennial visitation of New College, pp.32-33.

8. George Smeaton, 'The Pauline doctrine of the righteousness of faith', in *The British and Foreign Evangelical Review*, Vol. XI, No. XXXIX, Art. X (January, 1862), p.192. This is reproduced more or less verbatim in Smeaton's *The Doctrine of the Atonement as Taught by the Apostles* (1870), p.108.

9. PDGAFCS, May 1863, Report XXI, Report of committee on quinquennial visitation of New College, p.10. Smeaton's answers to questions raised with him in the visitation are found on pages 8 to 10 of this re-

port and provide the fullest detail of various aspects of his course at New College that is to be found in any such report.

10. *The Scotsman*, Monday, 30 May 1864, p.6. See also the report of the college committee to the General Assembly, May 1864, Report No. XXII, p.1. This raised George Smeaton's salary to £400 per annum. In an education committee report in 1862 it was noted that his salary at that point was £350.

11. PDGAFCS, May 1885, Report V.B., Report of commission on quinquennial visitation of the New College, p.15. Statement by Professor Smeaton.

12. Kenneth R. Ross, *Church and Creed in Scotland: The Free Church Case 1900-04 and its Origins* (Edinburgh, 1988), p.236.

13. W. Robertson Nicoll, *'Ian Maclaren': Life of the Rev. John Watson, DD* (London 1908, third edition), p.49. Watson (1850-1907) later became a minister in the English Presbyterian Church at Sefton Park in Liverpool. He apparently classified himself as a 'moderate' (Nicoll, *'Ian Maclaren'*, p.387).

14. Norman C. Macfarlane, *Rev. Donald John Martin* (Edinburgh, 1914), pp.34-35.

15. *The Free Church of Scotland Monthly*, 2 September 1889, p.279. In George Smeaton's time as a teacher in Edinburgh, some 950 students passed through New College (see Hugh Watt, *New College, Edinburgh: A Centenary History* [Edinburgh, 1946], pp.273-74).

16. See *The Scotsman*, Thursday, 7 November 1861, p.4; Thursday, 2 November 1876, p.3; Thursday, 6 November 1884, p.7. Presumably there were other occasions — unreported — when the introductory lecture fell to Smeaton. None of these lectures, to our knowledge, were published.

17. *The Scotsman*, Thursday, 22 April 1869, p.4. Thomas Jackson Crawford (1812-75) was professor of divinity at Edinburgh University (1859-75). He was an orthodox Calvinistic theologian who produced works of outstanding merit on *The Fatherhood of God* (1866), *The Atonement* (1871), and Baird lectures for 1874 on *The Mysteries of Christianity*. John Macleod says of Crawford that he 'made his name the best known of the divines of his church [Church of Scotland] as a sound and able theologian. His book on the atonement is of standard character' (*Scottish Theology*, Edinburgh, 1946, second ed., p.268.)

18. *Minutes* of the Free Presbytery of Glasgow, 19 February 1874 (cited in H. L. Goddard, 'The contribution of George Smeaton [1814-89] to theological thought', p.11). See also *The Scotsman*, 8 January 1874, p.6.

19. *The Free Church of Scotland Monthly*, 2 September 1889, p.279. This was written in a letter to the Rev. D. Hunter on 13 April 1889, the day before Smeaton's death.

Chapter 7

1. PDGAFCS, May 1859, p.22.
2. PDGAFCS, May 1859. Report No. 1, Report on the conversion of the Jews, p.17.
3. George Smeaton, *Improvement of a Revival Time* (Edinburgh c.1860), p.5.
4. Smeaton, *Improvement of a Revival Time*, p.6.
5. Smeaton, *Improvement of a Revival Time*, p.16.
6. George Smeaton, Introductory notice II, 'Suitableness of Erskine's writings to a period of religious revivals', in *The Beauties of the Rev. Ralph Erskine*, Samuel McMillan, ed. (Aberdeen, Edinburgh, London and Glasgow: A. Fullerton and Co., n.d. [1860]), p.xxxiii. Ralph Erskine (1685-1752) was a renowned preacher in Scotland in his day. He went into the Secession Church in 1737. It was said that his writings were long influential throughout the English-speaking world, and his sermons, full of God's love to sinners and offers of Christ in the gospel, were highly regarded. The *Beauties of Erskine* went through many editions in the nineteenth century.
7. Hugh Watt, *New College, Edinburgh: A Centenary History* (Edinburgh, 1946), p.119.
8. Letter held in New College Library.
9. In the Presbyterian church the Kirk Session is the ruling body with charge of the oversight of the local congregation. The minister is the moderator or chairman of the session. The elders are elected from among the male membership of the congregation (at least in the conservative churches). Where there is no minister in a congregation the presbytery appoints a minister, active or retired, from within the presbytery to act as moderator (or 'interim moderator') until a minister is elected.
10. The story is told in Thomas Maxwell, *St Catherine's in Grange 1866-1966* (Edinburgh, 1966), pp.28ff.

Chapter 8

1. John Macleod, *Scottish Theology* (Edinburgh, 1946, second ed.), p.288.
2. George Smeaton, *National Christianity and Scriptural Union* (Edinburgh, 1871), p.33. Smeaton is quoting the distinctive article of the United Presbyterian Church of Scotland on the subject.
3. As above.
4. PDGAFCS, 1843, p.12.
5. James Mackenzie and Robert Rainy, *Life of William Cunningham, DD* (Edinburgh, 1871), p.539.

6. *The Scotsman*, Thursday, 27 February 1868, p.7. Several 'overtures' were presented to that presbytery meeting. In the voting, Smeaton's overture in the event was withdrawn in favour of a very similar one put forward by Horatius Bonar which also pled for the discontinuance of the negotiations for union but at the same time 'recommending the cultivation of brotherly intercourse and co-operation in every work of faith and labour of love in which the negotiating churches can consistently with their principles unite'. In the end, however, this was defeated by an overture which advocated continuing the negotiations, even though it was clear by this time that there were irreconcilable differences at least on the matter of church/state relations. (See *The Scotsman*, Tuesday, 3 March 1868, pp.2-3). The debate was lengthy and heated, starting on the previous Wednesday evening (finishing at 11 p.m.), resuming on the Monday following (10:30 a.m.), and being concluded, after adjournments, at 2:30 a.m. on the Tuesday morning! Such was the intensity of church debates over controversial issues in those days.

7. James MacGregor, 'The question of principle now raised in the Free Church specially regarding the atonement' (Edinburgh, 1870), 76pp.

8. Amyraldism [or Amyraldianism] is the name given to some distinctive views of Moïse Amyraut, or Amyraldus (1596-1664). In relation to the decrees of God and consequently the reference of the atonement, Amyraut's thought was that by a universal decree God gave Christ as Mediator for the whole human race inclusively. Foreseeing, however, that not all would actually come to faith in Christ, by a subsequent decree — a special decree — God is said to elect some to receive the gift of faith. This allowed it to be said that Christ died for all men — hypothetically — though in fact only the elect will be saved. George Smeaton deals with Amyraldism in his volumes on the atonement. See *Christ's Doctrine of the Atonement* (1871, second ed.), pp.468-72; and *The Apostles' Doctrine of the Atonement* (1870), pp.540-43. Among more modern writers, Robert L. Reymond deals well with this aberration of Calvinism in his book, *A New Systematic Theology of the Christian Faith* (Nashville, 1998), pp.475-79.

9. Ian Hamilton, *The Erosion of Calvinist Orthodoxy* (Edinburgh 1990). See especially pp.91-101.

10. It is hardly mentioned by Charles G. McCrie in his authoritative study *The Church of Scotland: Her Divisions and her Reunions* (Edinburgh, 1901). McCrie's discussion of this controversy is found in pp.215-81. His pro-union bias is evident and, like so many in the church during that controversy, the differences over the issue of the extent of the atonement are sadly de-emphasized.

11. *The Scotsman*, Wednesday, 9 November 1870, p.6.

12. *The Scotsman*, Thursday, 10 November, 1870, p.7. Interestingly, although the voting for that motion was fifty-three to forty in the presby-

tery, the press report states that 'of the ministers a majority of one voted for the other side'!

13. George Smeaton, speech given 25 October 1870, Great Anti-Union Meeting in Glasgow (Glasgow: Free Church Defence Association, 1870), pp.6-8.

14. George Smeaton, *National Christianity and Scriptural Union* (Edinburgh, 1871), p.15.

15. Smeaton, *National Christianity*, p.54.

16. George Smeaton, preface to Thomas M'Crie's *Statement of the Difference &c.* Edinburgh, 12 June 1871. (Edinburgh: C. F. Lyon, 1871).

17. George Smeaton. *The Scottish Theory of Ecclesiastical Establishments* (Glasgow, 1875), pp.4-6.

18. C. G. M'Crie, *The Church of Scotland: Her Divisions and her Reunions* (Edinburgh 1901), pp.265-66.

19. 'Prayer in the present crisis', in *The Watchword*, 1 February 1873, pp.507-08. *The Watchword* was a publication which appeared between 1866 and 1873 for the purpose of defending distinctive Free Church principles. Its founder and editor was the Rev. James Begg. James Begg (1808-83) was minister of Newington Free Church, Edinburgh (1843-83). He was a prolific writer on the controversial issues of the day and effectively was the leader of the constitutional party in the Free Church at this period.

20. PDGFCS, 28 May 1873. Smeaton's speech is found on pp.154-57.

21. As above.

22. The sederunt is a period set for appointed business in an Assembly. A day will be broken up into various 'sederunts' in which specific business will be expected to be completed.

23. Candlish died 19 October 1873 after some years of ill health.

24. Macleod, *Scottish Theology*, p.307. The source for this statement cannot now be traced.

25. As mentioned elsewhere, this pamphlet has been reproduced in recent years by Still Waters Revival Books with the encouragement to readers to study carefully the arguments presented in favour of national religion and the truly Christian state.

26. *The Scotsman*, 15 April 1889, p.7. The term 'Establishment' here refers to the Church of Scotland denomination.

27. See *Institute Update*, the newsletter of the Christian Institute, Issue 6, Summer 2005, p.6.

28. Smeaton, speech given 25 October 1870, Great Anti-Union Meeting in Glasgow (Glasgow: Free Church Defence Association, 1870), pp.4-5.

29. Smeaton, *National Christianity*, pp.49-50.

30. Smeaton, speech given at Great Anti-Union Meeting in Glasgow, p.5.

31. Kenneth R. Ross, *Church and Creed in Scotland: The Free Church Case 1900-04 and its Origins* (Edinburgh, 1988), pp.151-52. Emphasis in the original.

Chapter 9

1. John Duncan (1796-1870) was the saintly professor of Hebrew and Oriental languages at New College, Edinburgh. His gravestone in the Grange Cemetery, Edinburgh, describes him as 'an eminent scholar and metaphysician, a profound theologian, a man of tender piety, and of a lowly and loving spirit'. Smeaton was chief mourner at the funeral of Dr Duncan.

2. John Macleod, *Scottish Theology* (Edinburgh, 1946, second ed.), p.288. In his biography of Alexander Whyte, Freeland Barbour wrote: 'Dr Davidson's widest influence was mediated through his pupils, especially Robertson Smith, Elmslie, Harper, and George Adam Smith.' (G. F. Barbour, *The Life of Alexander Whyte* [London, 1925, seventh ed.], p.107).

3. James MacGregor, *Studies in the History of Christian Apologetics* (Edinburgh, 1894), p.269. MacGregor, though conservative in theology and in matters of biblical criticism, took a weak position in the Robertson Smith case. See the author's article on 'Professor MacGregor, Dr Laidlaw and the case of William Robertson Smith' in *The Evangelical Quarterly*, Vol. XLVIII, No. 1, January-March 1976, pp.27-39.

4. PDGAFCS, May 1877. Report V.A., special report of the college committee on Professor Smith's article 'Bible', appendix IV, p.30.

5. A. C. Cheyne, *The Transforming of the Kirk* (Edinburgh, 1983), p.47.

6. Macleod, *Scottish Theology*, p.288. The source of this anecdote is not provided. In neither David Brown's biography of Duncan nor James Strahan's biography of Davidson are there any references to altercations or discussions between Smeaton and Davidson on this issue.

7. J. S. Black and G. W. Chrystal, *William Robertson Smith* (London, 1912), p.200.

8. As above.

9. Black and Chrystal, *William Robertson Smith*, p.201.

10. Quoted in 'The fault lines of faith', chapter twelve of Gordon Kempt Booth, 'William Robertson Smith: The scientific, literary and cultural context from 1866 to 1881' (PhD thesis, University of Aberdeen, 1999). This can be found on the website of GKB Enterprises: http://www.gkbenterprises.fsnet.co.uk/thesis/ch12.htm

11. As above.

12. PDGAFCS, May 1877. Report V, Appendix IV, p.31.

13. As above.

14. PDGAFCS, May 1877. Report V, Appendix IV, p.32.
15. PDGAFCS, May 1877. Report V, Appendix IV, p.33.
16. PDGAFCS, May 1877. Report V, Appendix IV, p.34.
17. R. L. Dabney, *Discussions: Evangelical and Theological*, (London, 1967 [1890]), vol. 1, p.401.
18. E. J. Young, *Thy Word is Truth*, (London, 1963), p.194.
19. N. M. deS. Cameron, *Biblical Higher Criticism and the Defence of Infallibalism in Nineteenth-Century Britain*, (Ontario, 1987), pp.261ff.
20. PDGAFCS, May 1877, Report V.A., Appendix IV, p.35.
21. PDGAFCS, May 1877, Report V.A., Appendix IV, p.37.
22. PDGAFCS, May 1877, Report V.A., Appendix IV, p.39. David Brown (1803-97), biographer of 'Rabbi' Duncan, was a man of conservative sympathies in biblical studies. He was perhaps best known as contributor to the Jamieson, Fausset and Brown *Commentary on the Whole Bible* (1871).
23. In ecclesiastical terms, a 'libel' is a formal charge against an individual. It may be raised by an individual or a church court (in the Presbyterian church). It will refer to some fault in doctrine or life. The individual minister (or professor) receiving this will be able to defend himself against it in the various church courts. A libel does not presume guilt. It is a means of establishing guilt, or innocence, in relation to the charge made.
24. Norman L. Walker, *Chapters from the History of the Free Church of Scotland* (Edinburgh, 1895), p.281.
25. PDGAFCS, May 1879, pp.90-91.
26. George Smeaton, *The Doctrine of the Holy Spirit* (Edinburgh, 1889, second ed.), p.408.
27. Smeaton, *The Doctrine of the Holy Spirit*, p.409.
28. John O'Neill in David F. Wright and Gary D. Badcock (ed.), *Disruption to Diversity: Edinburgh Divinity 1846-1996* (Edinburgh 1996), p.78.
29. Dabney, *Discussions: Evangelical and Theological*, p.401.
30. Dabney, *Discussions: Evangelical and Theological*, p.404. It was this book of Robertson Smith's which, in part at least, Alexander Moody Stuart sought to address in *The Bible True to Itself*, published in 1884.
31. Rousas J. Rushdoony, *Freud* (Philadelphia, 1965), p.21.
32. N. P. Madsen, 'Atonement and pneumatology: A study in the theology of George Smeaton', PhD thesis (University of St Andrew's, 1974), p.81.
33. Madsen, 'Atonement and pneumatology', p.83.
34. Madsen, 'Atonement and pneumatology', p.87.
35. Madsen, 'Atonement and pneumatology', pp.87-88.
36. *In Memoriam: Sermons Preached in Buccleuch Free Church, Sabbath, 21 April 1889, on the Death of the Rev. George Smeaton, DD* (Edinburgh, 1889), p.40.

37. For a brief summary of Smeaton's views of revelation and inspiration see chapter eleven of this book, pp.129-36.
38. A. Moody Stuart, *The Bible True to Itself* (London, 1884), p.187.
39. Kenneth R. Ross, *Church and Creed in Scotland: The Free Church Case 1900-04 and its Origins* (Edinburgh, 1988), pp.222-23.
40. C. H. Spurgeon, *The Sword and the Trowel* (London, 1889), p.634. The two professors to whom he referred were A. B. Bruce and Marcus Dods.
41. A. C. Cheyne, *The Transforming of the Kirk* (Edinburgh, 1983), p.57.
42. Macleod, *Scottish Theology*, p.289. It is of note that *The British Weekly*, in reporting the election of Marcus Dods to the Chair vacated by George Smeaton in New College, records that Thomas Smith, along with several others, went as far as to protest at Dods' appointment. See *The British Weekly*, Friday, 31 May 1889.
43. See James Robertson's Baird Lectures for 1889, *The Early Religion of Israel* (Edinburgh, 1892), and W. L. Baxter's *Sanctuary and Sacrifice: A Reply to Wellhausen* (London, 1895).
44. Donald Maclean, *Aspects of Scottish Church History* (Edinburgh, 1927), pp.170-71.
45. See Nicholas R. Needham, *The Doctrine of Holy Scripture in the Free Church Fathers* (Edinburgh 1991).

Chapter 10

1. For James MacGregor's 'Memorial' see PDGAFCS, Assembly Papers, May 1869, pp.152-61 under 'cases'.
2. James Gibson (1799-1871) was a doughty champion of Free Church orthodoxy. He was professor of systematic theology in the Free Church College in Glasgow (1856-71). Among other things he published *The Public Worship of God: Its Authority and Modes* (Glasgow, 1869), to counter the 'hymns' movement in the Free Church.
3. Hugh Martin (1821-85) was one of the outstanding theologians of the Free Church. He was responsible for many volumes which have been reprinted in recent years, such as *The Shadow of Calvary*, *The Abiding Presence*, *The Atonement*, *Jonah* and several others. He also wrote many articles and booklets on the hymns issue and articulately argued the case in the General Assembly.
4. The sad story of what occurred in the Grange Free Church at that time is told in *The Signal*, 1 May 1884, pp.152-59. *The Signal* was the organ of the Free Church Defence Association, an association of concerned constitutionalists within the Free Church.
5. George Smeaton, *The Doctrine of the Holy Spirit* (London, 1974, [1889, second ed.]), pp.29-30.

6. John M'Ewan, *Instrumental Music: A Consideration of the Arguments For and Against its Introduction into the Worship of the Free Church of Scotland* (Edinburgh, 1883).

7. Gysbertus Voetius (1588-1676) was a Dutch theologian. In 1611 he became pastor of Blymen, from where in 1617 he returned to Heusden. In 1619 he played an influential part in the Synod of Dort (or Dordt), and in 1634 was made professor of theology and Oriental science at Utrecht.

8. George Smeaton, preface to M'Ewan, *Instrumental Music*.

9. William Cunningham, *The Reformers and the Theology of the Reformation* (Edinburgh, 1862), pp.31-32. In 1967 the Banner of Truth Trust reprinted this posthumously produced volume in which the article had been reproduced.

10. The debate between these two great Free Church stalwarts in 1874 and 1875 has been recently reproduced in *Evangelism, A Reformed Debate* (James Begg Society, 1997).

11. See, for example, Iain H. Murray, *Should the Psalter Be the Only Hymnal of the Church?* (Banner of Truth Trust, 2001, 32pp.) and Malcolm H. Watts, *God's Hymnbook for the Christian Church* (James Begg Society, 2003, 64pp.; a substantial response to Murray's book). On the matter of instrumental music, see the interesting work of the American Reformed Baptist John Price, in his *Old Light on New Worship* (Avinger, Texas, 2005). These issues have not been confined to Scottish Presbyterians!

12. To this day (2007) that congregation has continuously adhered to unaccompanied psalm singing in public worship. The minister and congregation adhered to the Free Church in 1900 when the majority of the Free Church went in to a union with the United Presbyterian Church.

Chapter 11

1. John Macleod, *Scottish Theology* (Edinburgh, 1946, second ed.), p.288.

2. George Smeaton, *Memoir of Alexander Thomson of Banchory* (Edinburgh, 1869), p.vi.

3. George Smeaton, 'The basis of Christian doctrine in divine fact' (Aberdeen, 1854), p.19.

4. Smeaton, 'The basis of Christian doctrine', p.20.

5. George Smeaton, *The Doctrine of the Holy Spirit* (Edinburgh, 1889, second ed.), p.407.

6. George Smeaton, introductory note to *On the Inspiration of the Old and New Testaments: A Chapter from Thomas Chalmers* (Edinburgh, 1879), pp.1-2. Much of what Smeaton says here he reproduced in the

second edition of *The Doctrine of the Holy Spirit* (1889) in the section of his historical survey entitled 'Inspiration of the Spirit as at present discussed' (pp.406-08).

7. Smeaton, *The Doctrine of the Holy Spirit* (second ed.), p.146. Capitalization is Smeaton's.

8. Smeaton, *The Doctrine of the Holy Spirit* (second ed.), p.147.

9. Smeaton, *The Doctrine of the Holy Spirit* (second ed.), see pp.146-74.

10. Smeaton, *The Doctrine of the Holy Spirit* (second ed.), p.152. Italics are Smeaton's.

11. Smeaton, *The Doctrine of the Holy Spirit* (second ed.), p.173. Capitalization is Smeaton's. 'Theopneustic' is from the Greek word *theopneustos* meaning 'inspired', 'God-breathed', as found, for example, in 2 Tim. 3:16.

12. Smeaton, *The Doctrine of the Holy Spirit* (second ed.), p.174.

13. Smeaton, *The Doctrine of the Holy Spirit* (second ed.), pp.406-12.

14. Smeaton, *The Doctrine of the Holy Spirit* (second ed.), p.406.

15. As above.

16. N. P. Madsen, 'Atonement and pneumatology: A study in the theology of George Smeaton,' PhD thesis (University of St Andrews, 1974), p.237.

17. Smeaton, *The Doctrine of the Holy Spirit* (second ed.), p.147. It is interesting to note that this is part of two additional paragraphs added to the third lecture in the second edition of the work.

18. The Revised Version New Testament appeared in 1881 and the Old Testament in 1884. The whole Revised Version first appeared in 1885.

19. The New Testament text behind the Revised Version leant heavily on the new textual theories propounded concurrently by B. F. Westcott and F. J. A. Hort in their *The New Testament in the Original Greek* (New York, 1881).

20. Smeaton, *The Doctrine of the Holy Spirit* (second ed.), pp.129-30.

21. Smeaton, *The Doctrine of the Holy Spirit* (second ed.), p.133 (p.125 in the first edition).

22. Smeaton, *The Doctrine of the Holy Spirit* (second ed.), p.127. Smeaton quotes Dean J. W. Burgon's *Revision Revised*, which first appeared in 1883 and constituted a salvo against the newly published Revised Version New Testament. John William Burgon (1813-88) became the Dean of Chichester. He was a critic of Westcott and Hort and an advocate of the traditional text, which he valiantly sought to defend.

23. Smeaton, *The Doctrine of the Holy Spirit* (second ed.), p.409.

24. Smeaton, *The Doctrine of the Holy Spirit* (second ed.), p.411.

Chapter 12

1. George Smeaton, *The Doctrine of the Atonement as Taught by Christ Himself* (Edinburgh, 1871, second ed.), p.1.
2. Smeaton, *The Doctrine of the Atonement as Taught by Christ Himself* (second ed.), p.viii.
3. Smeaton, *The Doctrine of the Atonement as Taught by Christ Himself* (second ed.), p.23.
4. George Smeaton, *The Doctrine of the Atonement as Taught by the Apostles* (Edinburgh, 1870), p.v.
5. As above.
6. Smeaton, *The Doctrine of the Atonement as Taught by the Apostles*, p.426.
7. H. L. Goddard, 'The contribution of George Smeaton (1814-89) to theological thought,' PhD thesis (University of Edinburgh, 1953), p.109.
8. The first edition of *Christ's Doctrine of the Atonement* has simply forty-eight straight sections without any arrangement into chapters. The arrangement and layout in the first edition are pervasively revamped for the second edition, which is forty-six pages longer.
9. Smeaton, *The Doctrine of the Atonement as Taught by Christ Himself* (second ed.), pp.415-96.
10. Smeaton, *The Doctrine of the Atonement as Taught by the Apostles*, p.177.
11. Smeaton, *The Doctrine of the Atonement as Taught by Christ Himself* (second ed.), p.23.
12. Smeaton, *The Doctrine of the Atonement as Taught by Christ Himself* (second ed.), p.45.
13. Smeaton, *The Doctrine of the Atonement as Taught by Christ Himself* (second ed.), p.48.
14. Goddard, p.179.
15. As above.
16. Smeaton, *The Doctrine of the Atonement as Taught by Christ Himself* (second ed.), pp.44-51.
17. Smeaton, *The Doctrine of the Atonement as Taught by Christ Himself* (second ed.), p.77.
18. Smeaton, *The Doctrine of the Atonement as Taught by Christ Himself* (second ed.), p.60. Italics in the original.
19. Goddard, pp.100, 179.
20. Goddard, p.101.
21. Smeaton, *The Doctrine of the Atonement as Taught by Christ Himself* (second ed.), pp.182-86.
22. Smeaton, *The Doctrine of the Atonement as Taught by Christ Himself* (second ed.), p.182.

23. Smeaton, *The Doctrine of the Atonement as Taught by the Apostles*, p.341.
24. Smeaton, *The Doctrine of the Atonement as Taught by Christ Himself* (second ed.), p.183.
25. As above.
26. Smeaton, *The Doctrine of the Atonement as Taught by Christ Himself* (second ed.), pp.376-77.
27. Smeaton, *The Doctrine of the Atonement as Taught by Christ Himself* (second ed.), p.380.
28. Smeaton, *The Doctrine of the Atonement as Taught by Christ Himself* (second ed.), p.400.
29. Smeaton, *The Doctrine of the Atonement as Taught by Christ Himself* (second ed.), p.401-407.
30. Smeaton, *The Doctrine of the Atonement as Taught by Christ Himself* (second ed.), pp.406-07.
31. Smeaton, *The Doctrine of the Atonement as Taught by Christ Himself* (second ed.), p.407.
32. Norman C. Macfarlane, *Rev. Donald John Martin* (Edinburgh, 1914), p.35.
33. M. A. Kinnear, 'Scottish New Testament scholarship and the atonement c.1845-1920', PhD thesis (University of Edinburgh, 1995), p.179. The third chapter of this thesis deals specifically with 'George Smeaton and the development of the Calvinist view of the atonement' (pp.124-79).
34. Kinnear, p.131.
35. John O'Neill in David F. Wright and Gary D. Badcock (ed.), *Disruption to Diversity: Edinburgh Divinity 1846-1996* (Edinburgh 1996), p.77. O'Neill, an Australian, was appointed in 1985. He acknowledges an indebtedness to Kinnear in his knowledge of Smeaton (p.78, n.22).
36. Smeaton, *The Doctrine of the Atonement as Taught by Christ Himself* (second ed.), pp.70-71.
37. Robert Nicole, quoted on the dust jacket of George Smeaton, *The Apostles' Doctrine of the Atonement* (Grand Rapids, Michigan: Zondervan, 1957 [reprinted]).

Chapter 13

1. The second edition of Smeaton's work on the Holy Spirit is forty-six pages longer that the first.
2. In our opinion, the first of the volumes on the atonement was Smeaton's finest piece of work.
3. *Theanthropic* is from two Greek words — *theos*, meaning 'God', and *anthropos*, meaning 'man'. The word is used to describe the person of

Christ the Redeemer as both 'God and man, in two distinct natures, and one person, for ever' (Westminster Shorter Catechism, answer 22).

4. George Smeaton, *The Doctrine of the Atonement as Taught by the Apostles* (Edinburgh 1870), p.390.

5. The review by A. A. Hodge is found in *The Presbyterian Review*, April 1883, pp.453-54. Samuel Horsley (1733-1806) was an English divine who became Bishop of Rochester (1793) and St Asaph (1802). His *Sermons*, from which this quotation comes, were printed after his death (1810-12). Horsley was a prolific scholar and writer.

6. William H. Goold, ed., *The Works of John Owen* (London, 1965 [1850]), vol. III, p.162.

7. Goold, p.175.

8. R. M. Shillaker, 'The federal pneumatology of Gorge Smeaton (1814-89)', PhD thesis (Highland Theological College, 2002), pp.191-92. Christology is that branch of theology that deals with the doctrine of Christ the Redeemer.

9. George Smeaton, *The Doctrine of the Holy Spirit* (Edinburgh, 1882, first ed.), p.1. In the second edition of this work in 1889, Smeaton omits the phrase, 'except where Puritan influences are still at work'.

10. As above.

11. *The Presbyterian and Reformed Review*, no. 6, April 1891, p.209.

12. J. R. Beeke, *A Reader's Guide to Reformed Literature* (Grand Rapids, 1999), p.23.

13. N. P. Madsen, 'Atonement and pneumatology: A study in the theology of George Smeaton', PhD thesis (University of St Andrews, 1974), p.1.

14. Smeaton, *The Doctrine of the Holy Spirit* (second ed.), p.276. Emphasis in the original.

15. Smeaton, *The Doctrine of the Holy Spirit* (second ed.), p.277.

16. *Free Church Pulpit, Volume III* (Perth: James Dewar & Sons, 1847).

17. Smeaton, *The Doctrine of the Holy Spirit* (second ed.), p.283.

18. See 'The Spirit in a religious awakening,' in Smeaton, *The Doctrine of the Holy Spirit* (second ed.), pp.282-90.

19. Smeaton, *The Doctrine of the Holy Spirit* (second ed.), p.414.

Chapter 14

1. John Macleod, *Scottish Theology* (Edinburgh, 1946, second ed.), pp.288-89.

2. This comment is found on the web site of Still Waters Revival Books: http://www.swrb.com/Puritan/reformation-bookshelf-CDs.htm

   The booklet itself is to be found in the twenty-fifth volume of the Reformation Bookshelf CDs, entitled 'Reformation civil government (1/2)'.

3. George Smeaton, Introductory notice II, 'Suitableness of Erskine's writings to a period of religious revivals', in *The Beauties of the Rev. Ralph Erskine*, Samuel McMillan, ed. (Aberdeen, Edinburgh, London and Glasgow: A. Fullerton and Co., n.d. [1860]), p.xxxviii.

4. Henry Darling, DD, (1823-91) was an American Presbyterian minister. Ordained in the Northern Presbyterian Church in 1847, after pastorates in New York and Philadelphia he became president of Hamilton College, Clinton, N.Y., in 1881. He was clerk of the General Assembly (1854-63) and moderator in 1881. *The Closer Walk* was a devotional volume on the believer's experience of sanctification. Strangely, there are no copies of this volume to be found in British libraries.

5. *Memorials of the Late Miss Agnes Aitken* (Edinburgh, 1882), p.6. Agnes Aitken was born in 1808 and 'fell asleep in Jesus' in 1879. The volume of her memorials is a rare item.

6. Johannes Evangelista Gossner (1773-1858) entered the Roman Catholic priesthood in 1804. His evangelical tendencies brought about his dismissal, and in 1826 he entered the ministry of the Lutheran Protestant Church. It is said that 'as minister of the Bethlehem church in Berlin (1829-46), he was conspicuous not only for practical and effective preaching, but for the founding of schools, asylums and missionary agencies.' See the entry in Wikipedia, the free encyclopaedia, at http://en.wikipedia.org/wiki/Johannes_Gossner

7. B. B. Warfield, *Calvin and Augustine* (Philadelphia, Pennsylvania, 1956), p.289.

8. William Hastie, *Theology as Science and its Present Position and Prospects in the Reformed Church* (Glasgow, 1899), pp.97-98. Hastie (1842-1903) was professor of divinity at Glasgow University (1895-1903).

9. George Smeaton, 'The basis of Christian doctrine in divine fact' (Aberdeen, 1854), p.24.

Chapter 15

1. John Duns (1820-1909) was professor of natural science in New College, Edinburgh (1864-1903) and for many years acted as secretary of the Senatus. He wrote several books on the relation of science to Christian faith and was biographer of Sir James Young Simpson, discoverer of the anaesthetic properties of chloroform.

2. *In Memoriam: Sermons Preached in Buccleuch Free Church, Sabbath, 21 April 1889, on the Death of the Rev. George Smeaton, DD* (Edinburgh, 1889), p.42.

3. *In Memoriam*, p.16.

4. Thomas Maxwell, *St Catherine's in Grange 1866-1966* (Edinburgh, 1966), pp.50-51.
5. For further details of Oliphant Smeaton, see *Who Was Who, 1897-1916*, p.656.
6. H. L. Goddard, 'The contribution of George Smeaton (1814-89) to theological thought,' PhD thesis (University of Edinburgh, 1953), p.15.
7. John Davidson (1870-1945) was born in Lochans Schoolhouse, Stranraer. He studied at New College and was ordained as colleague and successor to the Rev. W. H. Goold at Martyrs Free Church on George IV Bridge, Edinburgh, on 6 October 1896. He subsequently went in to the Union in 1900 and married Aileen Smeaton on 15 June 1905, just three weeks before he was inducted to the charge of Denny Dunipace United Free Church. (This became a Church of Scotland congregation in 1929). He demitted the charge in October 1936. W. H. Goold was, of course, his wife's grand-uncle!
8. John Davidson (1908-83) was ordained and inducted to the charge of West Calder Harwood in the Church of Scotland on 6 September 1935. He was translated to Sanquhar St Bride's on 5 July 1949, from which he retired on 31 October 1974. He had two sons — great-great grandsons of George Smeaton — Alexander Michael Davidson (b.1944) and George Cook Davidson (b.1946). There are no doubt many other great-great-grandchildren through Aileen's large family.

Chapter 16

1. Marcus Dods, *Recent Progress in Theology* (Edinburgh, 1889), p.5.
2. *In Memoriam: Sermons Preached in Buccleuch Free Church, Sabbath, 21 April 1889, on the Death of the Rev. George Smeaton, DD* (Edinburgh, 1889), pp. 39-40.
3. See William Knight, *Some Nineteenth-Century Scotsmen* (Edinburgh and London, 1903), p.109.
4. John Macleod, *Scottish Theology* (Edinburgh, 1946, second ed.), p.289.
5. See, for example, George Smeaton, *The Doctrine of the Atonement as Taught by Christ Himself* (second ed.), p.23: 'Our plan leads us to proceed in an exegetical way, and not to argue from general principles or from mere dogmatic grounds.'
6. Macleod, *Scottish Theology*, p.289. Macleod does not provide the source of the statement attributed to James MacGregor.
7. Alexander Stewart and J. Kennedy Cameron, *The Free Church of Scotland: The Crisis of 1900* (Edinburgh, 1989 [1910]), p.31.

8. *Minutes* of the Kirk Session of Newington Free Church, 7 May 1889. A copy of a handwritten extract of this document is in the possession of the author.

9. 'Tribute to the memory of the late Professor Smeaton, DD', Free Church Defence Association. A copy of this handwritten tribute is in the possession of the author.

10. PDGAFCS, 4 June 1889, pp.46-47.

11. *The Free Church of Scotland Monthly*, 2 September 1889, p.279.

12. *In Memoriam*, pp.14-15.

13. George Smeaton, 'The faithful labourer's reward in heaven', a sermon [on Dan. 12:3] preached in the Free West Church, Aberdeen, on Sabbath, 5 May 1872, being the Sabbath after the funeral of the Rev. Alex. D. Davidson, DD, late minister of that church (Aberdeen, 1872), pp.23-24.

14. George Smeaton, 'The confessing of Christ before men, and the promised reward', a sermon preached in Newington Free Church, Edinburgh, on the occasion of the death of the Rev. James Begg, DD, on the afternoon of Sabbath, 7 October 1883 (Edinburgh, 1883), p.32.

Select bibliography

The published writings of George Smeaton

1. Printed sermons and lectures

1. 'The Lord's jealousy against backsliders consistent with his unchanging love', *Free Church Pulpit* (Perth: James Dewar and Son, 1845), vol. I, pp. 587-97.

2. 'A witnessing church — a church baptized with the Holy Ghost' (Perth: James Dewar and Son, 1846). This sermon was also reproduced in the *Free Church Pulpit* (Perth: James Dewar and Son, 1847), vol. III.

3. 'Necessary harmony between doctrine and spiritual life: being an introductory lecture, delivered on the 9th November 1853 to the Free Church students attending the Divinity Hall at Aberdeen' (Aberdeen: A. Brown; Edinburgh: Johnstone & Hunter, 1853).

4. Introductory lecture, winter 1853-54, on the origin, objects and necessity of the Association [Aberdeen Reformation Society] (Aberdeen: Stevenson, 1853).

5. 'Basis of Christian doctrine in divine fact: with particular reference to the modern realistic development of theology, being an introductory lecture, delivered at the opening of the Free Church divinity hall, Aberdeen, on Tuesday, 7 November 1854' (Aberdeen: A. Brown; Edinburgh: Johnstone & Hunter, 1854).

6. 'The real presence of Christ in the midst of his people', a sermon [on Rev. 2:1] preached before the Free Provincial Synod of Aberdeen, on Tuesday, 8 April 1856 (Aberdeen: Davidson, 1856).

7. Great Anti-Union Meeting in Glasgow, 25 October 1870: Speech of Rev. Professor Smeaton of Edinburgh [Free Church Defence Association, Offices: 109 West George Street, Glasgow] (Glasgow: Dunn and Wright, 1870).

8. '"Union inadmissible on the basis proposed": being speeches delivered by members of the majority of ministers in the Free Presbytery of Edinburgh, on 8, 9 and 10 November 1870; with appendices' (Edinburgh: Duncan Grant, 1870), speech by Professor Smeaton, pp.48-59.

9. '"The faithful labourer's reward in heaven", sermon [on Dan. 12:3] preached in the Free West Church, Aberdeen, on Sabbath, 5 May 1872, being the Sabbath after the funeral of the Rev. Alex. D. Davidson, DD, late minister of that church' (Aberdeen: D. Wyllie & Son; A. & R. Milne; and John Smith, 1872), pp.3-23.
10. 'A faithful minister of Christ' [on Col. 1:7] in 'Sermons preached in Free St Matthew's Church, Bath Street, Glasgow, with special reference to the death of the Rev. Samuel Miller, DD, by the Rev. Professor Smeaton, DD, Edinburgh; the Rev. John Watson, MA, Sefton Park Church, Liverpool; and the Rev. Charles A. Salmond, MA, Free St Matthew's, Glasgow' (Glasgow: John N. Mackinlay, 1881), pp.5-17.
11. 'The confessing of Christ before men, and the promised reward' [on Matt. 10:32] in 'Sermons preached in Newington Free Church, Edinburgh, on the occasion of the death of the Rev. James Begg, DD, by Rev. John Kennedy, DD, and the Rev. Professor George Smeaton, DD, on Sabbath, 7 October 1883' (Edinburgh: James Gemmell, 1883), pp.19-32.

2. Books and pamphlets

1. *The Improvement of a Revival Time*, New Year's tract (Edinburgh: James Taylor, c.1860).
2. *The Doctrine of the Atonement as Taught by Christ Himself* (Edinburgh: T. & T. Clark, 1868; second edition, 1871). Reprinted: 1953 (Zondervan); 1991 (Banner of Truth Trust); 2001 (Sovereign Grace Publishers). Published in the 1970s in the USA by Sovereign Grace Publishers, bound in one volume with *The Doctrine of the Atonement as Taught by the Apostles*.
3. *Memoir of Alexander Thomson of Banchory* (Edinburgh: Edmonston and Douglas, 1869).
4. *The Doctrine of the Atonement as Taught by the Apostles* (Edinburgh: T. & T. Clark, 1870). Reprinted: 1957 (Zondervan); 1979 (Alpha); 1988 (Hendrickson); 1991 (Banner of Truth Trust); 2001 (Sovereign Grace Publishers).
5. *National Christianity and Scriptural Union* (Edinburgh: Johnstone, Hunter & Co., 1871).

6. *The New Scheme of Incorporation*, Free Church tracts, no. 3 (Edinburgh, 1871).
7. *The Scottish Theory of Ecclesiastical Establishments and How Far the Theory is Realized.* An address to the Glasgow Conservative Association, 13 April 1875. (Glasgow: Association's Rooms; Edinburgh: Lyon & Gemmell, 1875).
8. *The Doctrine of the Holy Spirit* (Edinburgh: T. & T. Clark, 1882). Reprinted: 1958 (twice); 1961 (Banner of Truth Trust). Second edition, 1889. Reprinted: 1974; 1980; 1988; 1997 (Banner of Truth Trust).

3. Prefaces and introductions

1. Introductory notice on the 'Suitableness of Erskine's writings to a period of religious revivals', in *The Beauties of the Rev. Ralph Erskine*, Samuel McMillan, ed. (Aberdeen, Edinburgh, London and Glasgow: A. Fullerton and Co., n.d. [1860]).
2. Prefatory note to *Outlines of Discourses by the Late Rev. James Stewart, Aberdeen* (Edinburgh: Andrew Elliot, 1860).
3. Prefatory note to *Lord's Day*, by Johannes Gossner (London: T. Nelson and Sons, 1860).
4. Prefatory note to *Means and Methods to be Adopted for a Successful Ministry: Being an Introduction to Dr Spencer's 'Pastor's Sketches'*, by John Angell James. (Birmingham: Hudson and Son, 1861).
5. Preface to *The Closer Walk, or, the Believer's Sanctification*, by Henry Darling, DD (Edinburgh: Andrew Elliot, 1862).
6. Preface to '"Statement of the difference between the profession of the Reformed Church of Scotland, as adopted by the seceders, and the profession contained in the New Testimony and other Acts, lately adopted by the General Associate Synod: particularly on the power of the civil magistrate respecting religion, national reformation, etc.", by the late Thomas M'Crie, DD (1807)' (Edinburgh: C. F. Lyon, 1871).
7. Introductory note to 'On the inspiration of the Old and New Testaments: a chapter from Thomas Chalmers' (Edinburgh: Andrew Elliot, 1879).
8. Prefatory note to 'The inspiration and circulation of the Bible', by the Rev. William Fergusson (London: Elliot Stock, 1880).

9. Preface to *Memorials of the Late Miss Agnes Aitken* (Edinburgh: James Taylor, 1882).
10. Preface to *Instrumental Music: A Consideration of the Arguments For and Against its Introduction into the Worship of the Free Church of Scotland*, by the Rev. John M'Ewan (Edinburgh: James Gemmell, 1883).

4. Magazine articles

George Smeaton was editor of *The British and Foreign Evangelical Review*, in succession to William Cunningham, from 1860 to 1863. During that time and earlier he would have been responsible for many articles in the *Review*. Unfortunately, articles during that period were not attributed. The articles from the *Review* listed here have been picked up principally from notes in the appendix to the second edition of Smeaton's *The Doctrine of the Atonement as Taught by Christ Himself* (1871). In the case of articles listed in numbers 3, 7 and 8 below, there is a strong likelihood that these were from Smeaton's pen.

1. 'Immanuel: A discourse', in *The Scottish Christian Herald*, vol. II, second series, 4 January – 26 December 1840, pp.617-22.
2. 'Augustus Neander — His influence, system and various writings', in *The British and Foreign Evangelical Review*, vol. II, art. VI, September 1853, pp.701-39.
3. 'Old orthodoxy, new divinity and Unitarianism', in *The British and Foreign Evangelical Review*, vol. VII, no. XXIII, art. VIII, January 1858, pp.168-99.
4. 'Anselm and his theory of the atonement', in *The British and Foreign Evangelical Review*, vol. VIII, no. XXX, art. XI, October 1859, pp.918-56.
5. 'The theory of an incarnation without a fall', in *The British and Foreign Evangelical Review*, vol. X, no. XXXV, art. IV, January 1861, pp.80-96.
6. 'Oxford essayists', in *The British and Foreign Evangelical Review*, vol. X, no. XXXVI, art. X, April 1861, pp.407-30.
7. 'False theories of the atonement — McLeod Campbell and Baldwin Brown', in *The British and Foreign Evangelical Review*, vol. X, no. XXXVII, art. III, July 1861, pp.532-53.

8. 'Introduction to Romans', in *The British and Foreign Evangelical Review*, vol. X, no. XXXVII, art. VII, July 1861, pp.607-23.

9. 'The Pauline doctrine of the righteousness of faith', in *The British and Foreign Evangelical Review*, vol. XI, no. XXXIX, art. X, January 1862, pp.192-206. The substance of this article was reproduced in expanded and amended form in Smeaton's *The Doctrine of the Atonement as Taught by the Apostles* (Edinburgh, 1870), pp.106-26.

10. 'Dr Cunningham's theological works', in *The British and Foreign Evangelical Review*, vol. XI, no. XL, April 1862, pp.480-84.

11. 'The atoning blood', in *The Christian Treasury*, 1 February 1871, pp.73-75. From Professor Smeaton's able, learned, and exhaustive volume on the atonement (Edinburgh: T. & T. Clark, 1870). Our extract is from the last section, 'The testimony of John in the Apocalypse'.

12. 'The true preacher', in *The Christian Treasury* (Edinburgh: Johnstone, Hunter, & Co., 1872), pp.253-57.

13. 'Faith', article in *The Imperial Bible Dictionary* (London: Blackie & Son, 1886 [1864-1866]), pp.274-76.

Special studies: Works by other authors

1. Homer Lehr Goddard, 'The contribution of George Smeaton (1814-89) to theological thought' (PhD thesis, University of Edinburgh, 1960).

2. Norman Paul Madsen, 'Atonement and pneumatology: A study in the theology of George Smeaton' (PhD thesis, University of St Andrews, 1974).

3. Malcolm Andrew Kinnear, 'George Smeaton and the development of the Calvinist view of the atonement', chapter 3 (pp.124-79) in 'Scottish New Testament scholarship and the atonement' (PhD thesis, University of Edinburgh, 1996).

4. Robert Mark Shillaker, 'The federal pneumatology of George Smeaton (1814-89)' (PhD thesis, Highland Theological College, 2003).